Last Boat
to Yokohama

THE LIFE AND LEGACY OF
BEATE SIROTA GORDON

Nassrine Azimi & Michel Wasserman

WITH A FOREWORD BY
BEATE SIROTA GORDON

THREE ROOMS PRESS
NEW YORK

ACKNOWLEDGMENTS

*My gratitude to my mother Azar J. Azimi, for her love and gentle presence.
And to Chang Li Lin, Susan Dewhirst, and Kristin Newton, for their
friendship and generous advice.*

—*Nassrine Azimi*

Last Boat to Yokohama: The Life and Legacy of Beate Sirota Gordon
by Nassrine Azimi and Michel Wasserman

ISBN: 978-1-941110-18-8 (trade paper)
ISBN: 978-1-941110-19-5 (ebook)
Library of Congress Control Number: 2014951136

COVER AND INTERIOR DESIGN:
KG Design International
www.katgeorges.com

DISTRIBUTED BY:
PGW/Perseus
www.pgw.com

Three Rooms Press
New York, NY
www.threeroomspress.com

In Memoriam:

Joseph Gordon
(1919–2012)

and

Beate Sirota Gordon
(1923–2012)

Contents

Last Boat
to Yokohama

Foreword
by Beate Sirota Gordon

THIS BOOK IS ABOUT CROSS-CULTURAL EXCHANGE as my father, Leo Sirota, and I experienced it. It recounts my father's work as one of the first European professors of piano at the Imperial Academy of Music in Tokyo (as it was called in the 1930s). It also recounts my own experiences as Performing Arts Director of Japan Society and Asia Society, bringing traditional, folk, and modern performing arts from Asia to the United States from 1960 to 1992. In between, it describes some of my experience and work as a member of General Douglas MacArthur's staff in post-war Japan, as a participant in the drafting of the Japanese constitution. I hope this book succeeds in conveying to future generations the imperatives of universal human rights—including and especially women's rights—and the transformative power of the arts to encourage our nobler instincts.

Leo Sirota was a child prodigy from Kiev who moved to Vienna to study with Ferruccio Busoni. Looking at newspaper clippings of that time, it seems as if he had played in every major city in Europe. It was a hectic schedule and often took him away from his wife and child. His move in 1929 to Japan, with its leisurely pace, was therefore a dramatic change from the European milieu he had known (and must have seemed in many respects like being in an oasis). He taught at the Imperial Academy of Tokyo and privately, as well as concertizing in the Far East. In Japan, his concerts were sold out, and his teaching schedule at the Academy and to private students at his home was full. He also performed extensively on radio. His name became legendary. He was a true cultural pioneer. When a student mentioned that he was going to perform in a small provincial town, and therefore wouldn't have to practice very much, my father replied that, on the contrary, he would have to practice so much that he could penetrate the ignorance of his rural public with his brilliant technique and deep feeling for the music.

I started out as a monitor of Tokyo radio broadcasts for the CBS Listening Post in San Francisco, in the summer of 1942. This turned into the Foreign Broadcast Intelligence Service of the Federal Communications Commission. I translated broadcasts from Japanese, German, French, Russian, and Spanish. In 1944, I joined the Office of War

Information, as a writer and translator into Japanese of its propaganda broadcasts to Japan. In 1945, I moved to New York City and became an editorial researcher for *TIME* magazine. After the end of the war, in December 1945, I arrived in Japan to work as a research expert, for the Government Section of the GHQ SCAP (General Headquarters: Supreme Commander Allied Powers). I did research on women in politics and minor political parties, and worked on the political and economic purges, in addition to writing the women's rights article in the new Constitution of Japan. It was through my work in drafting the Constitution of Japan in 1946 that I first had the opportunity to introduce concepts from the West (though not necessarily from the United States) to Japan. I realized from reading so many constitutions how important it was to include human rights in this new constitution. In the nine days we worked on this document, we were exhilarated to be able to plant the seeds of democracy in Japan. I was thinking about the many Japanese women I knew, who did not have any rights at all under the old Meiji Constitution. I think most of the work we did then remains quite relevant today, as much for Japanese women as for women in other countries. I did my best to convince the Steering Committee to also include social welfare rights. I did not succeed. However, I did get approval for basic human rights.

I LEFT JAPAN FOR THE UNITED States in 1947 and married my coworker in GHQ, Lt. Joseph Gordon, in 1948. In 1954, I was named Education Director of Japan Society in New York City. Four years later, I became Japan Society's Director of Performing Arts. In 1970, I started working as Director of Performing Arts of Asia Society until I retired in 1991. Since 1995, I have been giving lectures on the constitution of Japan and on cultural exchange between Japan and the US. In 1997, my book *The Only Woman in the Room* was published.

What my father did parallels in some ways what I did later on in my career, but in the opposite direction. In his case, he brought West to East; in my case, I brought East to West. My late husband pointed out that this cultural exchange should not be too difficult a task, since all people have so much in common. We all have two hands and two feet, and one head. We all laugh at humor, we all cry when we are sad, we all want our children to succeed. In other words, we have many similarities to build on, and that was what we had to do. In my work I encountered many examples of the cultural similarities among different peoples. I was astounded when I saw martial arts exercises in Purulia, India, that I had learned as a student at the German School in Japan. I found a dance step similar to ballet's *bourrée* in China's Peking Opera. I found drums and flutes all over Asia, very much like their Western counterparts. At the beginning, I brought performing arts from Asia which were easy to communicate to a Western audience. I had excellent visual aids such as brochures, posters, and photographs, which helped in my efforts to make people appreciate the performance. But most importantly I brought the best performers who knew how to communicate their art. Of course, I also had difficulties, but fortunately I had learned from my father how to deal with such situations—calmly and patiently. Some performers wanted to bring flashy costumes to the US, thinking this would impress a Western audience. They feared that authenticity was too drab! It took a lot of persuading to convince them otherwise.

In the end, my husband was right. It is not that difficult to introduce one culture to another. But it can only be done by presenting the best of the alien culture, by explaining it and by demonstrating and highlighting that which we all have in common. My father did it, I did it.

—Beate Sirota Gordon
New York City, October 8, 2012

Beate

I FIRST MET BEATE SIROTA GORDON in November 2002, in New York. At the time I was in charge of a small team at the Geneva headquarters of the United Nations Institute for Training and Research (UNITAR), assigned the task of opening my institute's first Asia office in Hiroshima, Japan. We had recently held an international conference in Hiroshima on post-war rebuilding, and were looking for someone significant to write an introduction to a publication on the conference's proceedings.

The conference topic—a comparative study of the immediate post-war period in Japan, Korea, Vietnam, Cambodia, East Timor, and Afghanistan[1]—was

---

1 *Post-Conflict Reconstruction in Japan, Republic of Korea, Vietnam, Cambodia, East Timor and Afghanistan: Proceedings of an International Conference in Hiroshima, November 2002*, edited by Nassrine Azimi, Matt Fuller, Hiroko Nakayama, United Nations Press, New York and Geneva, 2003.

particularly timely. Those were the early days of the American-led occupation of Afghanistan. The consolidation phase had begun in earnest but was already struggling on multiple fronts. Still—barely a year after the collapse of the Taliban and the end of their mournful, brutal reign—those were also hopeful times and the writing of a new constitution for Afghanistan had become all the buzz, especially in the community of "nation builders." Throughout 2002, it became of paramount importance to get my hands on nearly everything about post-WWII Japan, particularly if it had to do with the constitution or civil rights. And, invariably, any serious study of post-war Japan and its constitution leads one sooner or later to Beate Sirota Gordon.

We corresponded, and when visiting New York City I called her to explain the findings of the conference, and also to say that I would love for her to write something for the book. She responded—the way she always responds—warmly, spontaneously, and pragmatically. "We cannot discuss all this on the phone—just come visit me"—were to be the simple words that commenced a deep and inspirational friendship.

I did go to visit Beate shortly thereafter. I had always loved Japan but that love was at best superficial and distanced; recently, however, my interest had deepened, and to me Beate's apartment was a veritable Ali Baba's cave. In those days she and Joe Gordon[2]—her elegant, erudite, and enormously witty husband from the Bronx—were living on Riverside Drive in the Upper West Side of New York, in one of those slightly run-down but sophisticated turn-of-the-century architectural gems. Though the apartment was not large, a grand piano stood in the living room and the walls were covered with the works of Shikō Munakata[3], whose extraordinary introduction to New York Beate had masterminded in 1959. We sat at a long wooden table in the dining room, covered with manuscripts and books, and talked about everything—Japan, Hiroshima, WWII, Asia Society, my land of birth in Iran, my adopted country of Switzerland. She came across as intellectually curious and politically engaged—a woman with clear values and independent opinions, which she expressed in a matter-of-fact way, but which were rarely disparaging about the people or institutions she disliked or disagreed with. She managed to be both courtly and informal at the

---

2 During the war, Joseph Gordon had been trained in Japanese at the military language school in Michigan. He was co-head of the interpreters pool of the Government Section at Supreme Command of the Allied Powers (SCAP) from 1945 to 1946. After marriage, Beate would take on her husband's family name, but would later on retrieve her maiden name as well, using the full Beate Sirota Gordon.

3 Celebrated woodblock printmaker (1903–1975). His bold creations are strongly influenced by Buddhist religious imagery and the folk traditions of his native northern Japan.

same time, with a most contagious laugh. It was hard to disagree with the historian John Dower, who in his seminal work *Embracing Defeat* described the Beate Sirota of the post-war years as ". . . spirited, idealistic, and remarkably cosmopolitan."[4] She had not changed much, I thought, and I took to her right away.

I did not know much about her past, yet as we worked through some documents at that very first encounter, I discovered the inveterate researcher and disciplined professional that Beate had always been. She answered my questions with precision and patience, and asked quite a few of her own with the same intense focus. Finally, she accepted my request to write the preface of the conference book.[5] We continued to keep in touch after my move to Hiroshima.

FROM EARLY ON, ONE OF THE most important programs of the UNITAR Asia office was the Hiroshima Fellowship for Afghanistan—an executive training series that has since become a reference in the field of human resource development.[6] The visits of the Afghan Fellows to Japan, and especially to Hiroshima, were

---

4 John W. Dower, *Embracing Defeat: Japan in the Wake of World War II*, W. W. Norton & Company, New York, 1999, p. 365.

5 The full text of the preface written by Beate appears on pp. 125–128.

6 The Hiroshima Fellowship for Afghanistan, one of UNITAR's long-standing executive series, started in 2003 with support of Hiroshima Prefecture, and continues to this day. It has trained hundreds of Afghan professionals thus far and established an alumni network that is considered one of the best in the country.

always moving as they observed a firsthand example of another nation risen from its wartime ashes. To these Afghan professionals and others in post-conflict countries, broken and exhausted after decades of war and bloodletting, struggling for a sense of renewal, the green and prosperous Hiroshima was a genuine source of encouragement.

Unlike many Western powers, Japan had no colonial baggage in Afghanistan. And, although still distrusted in many quarters of China, Korea, and Southeast Asia and resented for the brutality of its military in World War II, Japan was, and remains, well loved and respected in Western Asia and the Middle East. Its particular blend of East and West—highly successful as a technologically savvy country, yet able to retain its culture and traditions—continues to exercise great influence in that region.

As I learned and thought more about what Hiroshima actually meant or could mean for other countries emerging from war and conflict, Beate's work, too, seemed to be coming into sharper focus. The more I read by and about her, the better I understood the unique historical circumstances of her involvement in the drafting of the post-World War II Japanese constitution, including the significance of the women's rights clause she helped develop. But her place of prominence in history is not restricted to being a member of the team that drafted such an extraordinary constitution. After the war, and throughout her adult life, Beate grew to be a truly influential cultural figure, bridging relations between the United States and Japan through her work with New York's Japan Society and, later, with the Asia Society. To an uninformed, but eager-to-learn American audience, she introduced the best of Asia's artistic treasures and traditions—including those of its recent bitter enemy.

I knew from the start that I had met an exceptional person, and I wanted to find ways to distill and convey the essence of her work to new audiences. What she had accomplished over six decades was not merely historical record. Rather, her efforts were absolutely relevant to addressing contemporary global challenges as well—from those in Afghanistan and Iraq, to others in the United States itself. I was curious to find people of her caliber in our times, since clearly Beate's life story continues to resonate with all women who experience tyranny and war. And then there was the personal side—her values, her perseverance. Accidents of history and chance may have put her in the right place at the right time, but it was mostly by virtue of her upbringing and her personal qualities that she managed to overcome difficulties and turn them into something more universally meaningful.

Beate herself was always aware of a certain universal quality in her life and work, as she detailed—succinctly but eloquently—in a revelation about what the constitution of Japan meant to her:

> On a more subtle level, since 1947, the Japanese Constitution has brought profound changes to the mores of a once militaristic society, and has sown the seeds of democracy and equality. Critics insist that because of cultural differences and customs, the Constitution is not "Japanese" enough. Japan's experience has demonstrated, however, that in the end, people around the world are far more alike than they are different. They all want freedom, food, good health, education for their children, and happiness. Universal human rights know no boundaries. And those of us who have the privilege of enjoying these rights also have a responsibility to help others achieve the same goals. We must do so with idealism, passion, and the will to prevail. The alternatives are simply too grim to contemplate.[7]

In January 2011, I spent a week with Beate and Joe at their apartment in New York. We went through her archives and spent hours at the New York Public Library for the Performing Arts in Lincoln Center, viewing some of the videos of the performances she had brought to America. I realized there was a story to tell—of a father who had taken Western music to Japan, and his daughter, who had brought so much of Japan and Asia to the West.

---

7 *Post-Conflict Reconstruction . . ., op. cit.*, p. 4.

The story had to be told as one continuum. And it was clear, too—considering that my knowledge of the performing arts of Japan and Asia (and indeed the West) was limited—that I would not be able to tell it in full on my own.

It is at that point that serendipity intervened. In February 2011, on the way to the Japan Sea, I stopped in Kyoto to meet with Michel Wasserman, the former director of the Institut franco-japonais du Kansai and a scholar whose writings on Paul Claudel, the poet-ambassador of the 1920s and one of the most distinguished French envoys to Japan, I had read and admired. To my astonishment, I found someone not only deeply versed in the musical scene of 1930s Japan, but knowledgable about Leo Sirota as well. Furthermore, Michel had been so enchanted by a Noh performance he saw in 1971 at an American university, that he promptly left for Tokyo to embark on a career of researching Japanese traditional theater. He has lived in Japan ever since.[8] Our plan for the book, which took almost a year to take shape, seems in hindsight obvious: Michel would write about Leo and Beate's work with the performing arts, and I would write about Beate and the constitution—even if in many ways the two were intertwined. Japan would be at the center of it all—for both father and daughter.

---

8 It is truly ironic that this particular performance was, in fact, not organized by Beate, a rarity in 1971!

It is difficult to separate Beate's work with the Japanese constitution—a testament to her trust in the nobility of the Japanese people—with her later activities presenting and explaining the country's culture. When she started the latter work in the early 1950s, most Japanese were still living in dreadful economic conditions. Some six million soldiers had returned from the front, food was scarce, and shantytowns, beggars, and prostitutes were still common sights. Art was probably the last thing ordinary people were thinking about. One may well ask how, despite such bleak and desolate economic and social circumstances, was Japan able to come up with so much art, and how was Beate able to find it?

I believe that the same qualities that informed her work during and immediately following the war also marked her activities as a cultural bridge. For one, she had an impeccable eye for quality. Her parents were sophisticated and passionate artists. As an only child, Beate had gone almost everywhere with them—theater, dance, concerts, painting exhibitions. Such frequent exposure equipped her early in life with the ability to recognize brilliant art. Later, as she studied at Mills College in Oakland, California, during the war years, she served as an au pair in the home of none other than the distinguished twentieth-century French composer Darius Milhaud, gaining an even deeper understanding of musical culture. By early adulthood, there was practically no artistic discipline about which she did not have a learned opinion, or at least a basic understanding of its essentials.

Equally important, she had an inherent understanding of what was meant by "universal values." She recognized the importance of ensuring women's rights in a conservative society; she comprehended what types of artistic endeavors could move audiences and people anywhere, transcending nationality, background, or level of familiarity. Going through the program notes her staff had prepared for each of the performances she had brought from Asia—with obviously great financial resources but also with exquisite taste and pedagogical insight—one can easily see just how consistently her intent was to educate.

But I believe the most significant characteristic Beate brought to her work—during the war and the Supreme Command of the Allied Powers (SCAP) years, as well as during her later years as a cultural bridge—was a profound idealism. She was from the generation that had experienced war. She knew firsthand the devastations it could wreak, knew how it could turn brother against brother, how it could transform perfectly decent human beings into monsters. During the war she had become aware of the atrocities committed by the Japanese army across wide swaths of Asia. And, as a descendant of European Jews, she had lost family and friends to Nazi savagery. Though she was profoundly convinced of the wide gap between ordinary Japanese and their military rulers, she also knew—there was no hiding from it—that ordinary people, driven by the pressures of extraordinary circumstances, could become beasts.

Beate was not yet twenty-two when the war ended. Yet she believed then, and continued to believe till the end of her life, that the way to peace was for people to understand one another. Culture could provide the bridge to reconciling differences. She was intimately convinced of the transformational powers of art to improve humanity, to foster understanding, to encourage our nobler instincts. In this sense, she was a true daughter of her father and a role model for me and for millions of women who continue to benefit from and be inspired by her work, her courage, and her beautiful humanity.

Leo

In the Vienna of the 1920s, a little girl of four was to become the center of admiration for declaring to whomever would ask that Igor Stravinsky was her very favorite musician. She would have certainly heard her father, the virtuoso pianist Leo Sirota, practicing Stravinsky's notoriously difficult *Three Movements from Petrushka* for weeks at a time. The piece was so difficult that Arthur Rubinstein—to whom it was dedicated and who was originally slated to perform it—had ultimately withdrawn; one may never know if for any reason other than sheer terror!

Leo Sirota, who by that time had been living in Vienna for almost twenty years, was born Leiba Gershovitch in 1885 in Ukraine. His parents were originally from Kamianets-Podilskyi in Western Ukraine (a city that was later to acquire the tragic legacy of bearing witness to the horrific 1941 Shoah mass assassinations of Jews by gunshot).

From the beginning, "Leo" had to cope with the anti-Semitism that was poisoning Eastern European societies. The somewhat sinuous progression of his career—through the Kiev Conservatory, amidst the cosmopolitanism of the Viennese music scene where in the footsteps of his mentor Busoni he enjoyed a precocious fame and, finally, in his mid-forties, through his choice of artistic exile in Japan—can only be understood in the context of the somber political developments that marked his formative years and pursued him throughout much of his adult life.

Leo's profile was that of the typical child prodigy. He gave his first concert at the age of eight, and the following year entered the Imperial School of Music in Kiev, where one of his classmates was the future teacher of Vladimir Horowitz. In his first concert tour of Russia, at the age of ten, Leo is said to have so impressed the legendary pianist Paderewski that the latter tried, in vain, to persuade Leo's parents to send him to Paris to study under his direction. At barely fourteen, Leo had already become the chief piano accompanist of the Kiev Opera, accompanying the likes of the great Russian opera singer Feodor Chaliapin. Later, he would enter St. Petersburg Conservatory, from which he graduated in 1908.

Though his was an impeccable track record, Leo also experienced professional failure at a young age. In 1905, Leo, and other future musical greats Béla Bartók and Otto Klemperer, entered the Anton Rubinstein piano competition in Paris. They all lost to Wilhelm Backhaus. Leo was twenty, a critical age for a young instrumentalist. The shock of this failure is what may have led him to become the student of Ferruccio Busoni following his graduation from the conservatory.

Busoni was an exceptional virtuoso in the Lisztian tradition, as well as a talented modernist composer who very early on grasped the importance of the work of Bartók and Arnold Schoenberg. Busoni, who, since 1907, had been giving master classes in Vienna, was to have a deep influence on the musical and intellectual development of Leo, who became one of his favorite students. Busoni's admiration for his young disciple was so great that he dedicated the charming Mozartian transcription *Giga, Bolero e variazione* to him. The two enchanted all of musical Europe on December 18, 1910 at the Wiener Musikverein when they performed the two-piano version of Liszt's *Réminiscences de Don Juan* as well as the *Sonata in D major K.448* by Mozart. The master then proceeded to conduct the Tonkunstler Orchestra, accompanying his student in the monumental *Concerto in C major, Op. 39* for piano, orchestra, and male chorus, which he had created for himself as soloist in 1904. The piece—requiring almost seventy minutes of technical prodigy—is so imposing on the soloist that this act alone could be considered proof of the immense sentiments of mutual trust and admiration that united the two artists.

Had it not been for World War I, Leo's career might have progressed far more rapidly. Still, he was fortunate to be able to spend the war years in Vienna, thereby evading military conscription in Russia. Although a citizen of an enemy nation, he maintained a sufficient number of professional activities so that by the time he started his tours of European concert halls in the 1920s, he was an accomplished, though still relatively unknown, performer. Loyal to the teachings and philosophy of Busoni, Leo put his immense talents as much at the service of classical repertoire like Liszt's, as of more modern composers like Stravinsky, Schoenberg, Prokofiev, Korngold, and Marx—musicians whose works he would often include in both his solo performances and in concerts with orchestras.

During this time, Leo also frequently performed at the Salle Pleyel in Paris, at the invitation of his brother Pierre. A former pianist forced to give up his musical career due to stage fright, Pierre instead became a prominent impresario, managing some of the most talented artists of the time: performers of the caliber of the variety stars Mistinguett and Maurice Chevalier, the conductor Serge Koussevitzky, the actor Sacha Guitry, and the choreographer Michel Fokine. Guided from afar by the capable Pierre, Leo undertook a long concert tour of Russia and the Ukraine during 1927 and 1928. One performance led to another, and he journeyed as far as the eastern parts of the Soviet Union, finally arriving in Harbin, then the cosmopolitan musical center of Chinese Manchuria. In Harbin, the Japanese composer of Western music, Kosaku Yamada heard Leo play; he was so impressed by the pianist's rendition of *Petrushka* that he promptly asked Leo to cap his tour of the Far East with a few concerts in Japan.

Over five weeks, from November to late December 1928, Leo gave some sixteen concerts in music halls small and large in Tokyo and Osaka. Culturally astute, during one concert he dedicated the slow movement of Mozart's *Concerto K. 537 (Coronation)* to the newly enthroned Emperor Hirohito. For his last concert, in Tokyo's *Nihon Seinenkan*, Leo performed on a Yamaha piano—a delicate and endearing gesture from a great master of Western music at a time when it would not have occurred even to Japanese pianists themselves to play on any instrument other than a Bechstein or a Steinway!

And thus, Leo's first concert tour of Japan (which among many audiences revived memories of those given by Godowsky in 1922) was a great success, unanimously recognized as a major cultural event. It led to an invitation for a return performance in the autumn of 1929. After spending a short time back in Vienna, Leo once again boarded the Trans-Siberian railway, this time accompanied by his wife Augustine (the sister of the conductor Jascha Horenstein) and their only child, Beate, who was now nearly six years old.

Initially planning to visit for only six months, the couple ultimately stayed in Japan for seventeen years. It was quite exceptional at the time—when the length and difficulty of traveling to the Far East often meant severing contacts with Europe's musical scene—that a pianist of Leo Sirota's stature would undertake such a career move. Indeed, even before the rise of Hitler forced other Jewish musicians into exile, Leo seemed to have decided, at the age of forty-five, to forego a standard international career. In his case, world events soon proved his decision the right one: the New York Stock Market collapse in October 1929 coincided with the Sirota family's arrival in Tokyo and rendered his return to Europe—where the financial crisis soon extended—improbable; economic as well as political developments continued to deteriorate, especially in Austria, where inflation and unemployment resulted in right- and left-wing paramilitary groups fighting each other.

Meanwhile, in Japan, concerts gave way to more concerts and Leo, recognized as a great master, soon acquired many private students. In 1931, having already extended the provisional date of any return to Europe, he was formally invited to teach at the Imperial Academy of Music of Tokyo, a prestigious institution established on the Western model of musical education. Thus, in the same year that Japan's economy became increasingly strangled by the slowdown of textile exports to America, Leo and his family settled into a comfortable and fulfilling life in Tokyo.

Later, in September of the same pivotal year of 1931, Japan fabricated the Manchurian Incident, essentially allowing it to seize, for free, the natural resources that it no longer had the foreign currency to buy from China. An incorrigible optimist, Leo may not have realized that through this act of international piracy, his newly adopted country had started on an ill-fated path of diplomatic isolation, union with the authoritarian Axis powers, and ultimately the tragedies of Hiroshima and Nagasaki.

Rather, Leo remained focused on both his public and private teachings. According to the composer Alexandre Tansman, who visited the academy two years after Leo began teaching there, the Tokyo students were in no way less talented than those at the Paris Conservatory.

Leo also continued performing—but at his own pace and without the constant pressures of perpetual traveling he had experienced in Europe. He played chamber music with his longtime partner Robert Pollak, a Viennese violinist who had become a professor at the Academy due to Leo's support. He performed often as a soloist with the all-Japanese musicians of the New Symphony Orchestra, formed by the NHK Broadcasting Company, the national radio network established in 1925. He also recorded frequently for the radio, most notably Beethoven's complete piano sonatas, a rarity at that time.

In 1935, Hidemaro Konoye, the founding conductor of the New Symphony Orchestra—a high-ranking aristocrat who had studied conducting and composition in Germany—unexpectedly left his position. To the astonishment of all, he was replaced by the German conductor Joseph Rosenstock, a musical star of international fame. Rosenstock had once been in consideration to lead the Berlin Opera, but with Hitler's grip on power he had been sidelined. In 1933, he was assigned to direct the opera department of the *Jüdischer Kulturbund*, an institution created by Jewish performers, and cynically patronized by Goebbels, to allow Jewish artists to perform in Germany—but only for fellow Jews. Rosenstock had courageously shouldered this responsibility for almost three years, bringing much-needed comfort to increasingly desperate audiences. But the growing accumulation of insults, repressive measures and administrative indignities that would lead to *Kristallnacht* in 1938 and ultimately to the Final Solution, soon forced Rosenstock to contemplate departure. His initial idea was to return to the United States where in the past he had conducted the German repertoire at the Metropolitan Opera in New York, until he unexpectedly received an invitation from Tokyo to direct the New Symphony Orchestra for two years. He accepted without hesitation—immediately embarking on the Trans-Siberian railway in Moscow and arriving in Tokyo in August 1936.

Despite the torpid summer heat, the orchestra, in full, awaited his arrival at the train station—alongside an army of reporters. The musicians were surely flattered, and perhaps a little anxious, that such a renowned and reputedly difficult musical celebrity had agreed to lead them. Rosenstock, always forthright with his words, promptly proceeded to denounce the German government, declaring that the country was now a place "where music is crushed a little more each day. Even [Wilhelm] Furtwängler can no longer conduct."

His words did not fall upon deaf ears. The Embassy of the Third Reich in Tokyo, had been actively seeking to undermine Japan-based Jewish musicians since 1933 and had tried in vain to see its own candidates succeed the orchestra's resigning conductor. Now, under the pretext that the words of Rosenstock and activities of other Jewish musicians in Japan could negatively influence political relations between the two allies, the Embassy's Chargé d'Affaires, in the strongest of terms, asked the Japanese Ministry of Foreign Affairs for their immediate expulsion. In response, the Japanese Ministry cited the popularity of these musicians among the general public, stating that any action taken against them on the basis of their religion could backfire and give rise to feelings of solidarity and sympathy for all Jews.

Still, influenced by ongoing Nazi propaganda, and faced with the need to control a rush of European Jewish refugees to Japan-controlled Shanghai as well as its puppet state of Manchukuo, the Japanese government determined that it had to articulate an overall policy for dealing with the question of Jewish immigration. The government moved cautiously, concerned about provoking the United States—where anti-Japan sentiments were already strong—not wanting to jeopardize the chances of foreign investment in its newly acquired colonies. At the time, the Japanese government did not wish to cede to German pressure regarding its policy on the treatment of Jews. In Japan, the topic was not considered a priority. Ultimately, toward the end of 1938, the War Ministry developed an ad hoc policy, deciding that treatment of Jewish residents of Japan would be similar to that of all foreign residents of the country. The Jewish population would not be subjected to specific expulsion measures. On the other hand, Jewish individuals would no longer be encouraged to settle in Japan, China, or Manchuria "with the exception of investors and technicians which could be of specific utility" to the Empire—musicians of the rank of a Rosenstock or a Sirota would obviously be included in the latter category. That very same year, Leo celebrated ten years of residence in Japan, with a Chopin recital at the *Hibiya Kôkaidô*—a two-thousand-seat concert hall built in the late 1920s.

The start of the Pacific War—the theater of operations of which would remain for several years outside of Japan and which, in the beginning, had produced an endless array of maritime and territorial conquests—hardly slowed musical life across the country. On the contrary, the number of concerts at the *Hibiya Kôkaidô* with Rosenstock conducting the Radio Orchestra doubled as of 1940. As for Leo, 1942 was one of his busiest years. He was the designated soloist for the subscription concerts of the Tokyo Symphony, a second Japanese orchestra, under the direction of Manfred Gurlitt. He also performed in concert with Russian violinist Alexander Mogilevsky, a former partner of Rachmaninoff in pre-revolutionary Russia.

By late 1942, the war situation started to turn. Japan soon faced repeated defeat in the Battle of Midway and later in the Battle of Guadalcanal. The country's festive mood gradually soured and the feelings of exaltation at the wake of swift early victories began to fade. The high command of the army, which had envisaged a swift start to the peace negotiations based on early successes, now struggled to contain a counter-offensive and, potentially, an invasion.

Foreign residents still present in Japan—particularly those who did not support the Axis—were perceived by authorities as a potential fifth column. In October 1943, the Japanese Musical Culture Association issued a ban that prohibited native Japanese performers from appearing in any concerts with non-Axis artists. The policy applied to Jewish musicians of German origin who had been stripped of their nationality by the Nazis, as well as those who, like Leo, had been naturalized Austrians before becoming citizens of the Third Reich following the Anschluss. Already under contract for a Beethoven concert in Yokohama, Leo was forced at the last minute to ask one of his students to play in his place. In June 1944, after fifteen years in Japan as a concert pianist and a noted professor at the Academy of Music, his contract expired and was not renewed.

By then, the war had turned into a nightmare for Japan. In July 1944, at the Battle of Saipan—a tiny, but strategically important Micronesian island—the Japanese military division was entirely obliterated. Saipan also had the tragic distinction of witnessing the first collective suicides among civilian populations. Brainwashed by the Imperial Army and so terrified of what the "monstrous" Americans would do to them, ordinary people chose instead the promise of being honored, post mortem, as rightful combatants. Today, one can still visit the bleak sites of Suicide Cliff and Banzai Cliff in Saipan. There, entire Japanese families lined up in order of age from youngest to oldest, and pushed one another into the sea, killing themselves to avoid falling into the hands of the victorious enemy.

The strategic importance of Saipan and other Mariana Islands may explain the exceptional violence of the confrontations there and the hysteria among the participants. Those tiny island specks in the vast Pacific Ocean put major military and industrial sites in Japan—as well as most of its main cities—within the flying range of the American B-29 bomber, the aptly named Superfortress.

Within a year of their seizure of Saipan, the Americans upgraded the Japanese-built military airport on the small twin island of Tinian, building landing strips able to accommodate heavy bombers. It soon became the most active airport in the world, with some 20,000 bombing missions flying out to target numerous Japanese cities, filled with the wooden architecture which made them particularly vulnerable to aerial bombings. From March 9 through March 10, 1945, more than three hundred nighttime bombing missions devastated the industrial neighborhoods of Tokyo—most notably the flat areas to the east of the Imperial Palace. Some 1,700 tons of bombs incinerated the capital, killing more than 100,000 people in one night and making this single outing the deadliest of all of World War II. For three weeks Tokyo burned, and there were so many corpses that the *Hibiya Kôkaidô*, the concert hall where Leo had performed so often, was turned into a chapel. During another incendiary bombing in May, the Sirota house in the western residential quarters burned down entirely. When she went to look for her old home, Beate, who had left to study in the United States in 1938 and returned only at the end of 1945 as research staff at the Occupation headquarters, found only a single stone pillar that formerly stood at the entrance to the house. Fortunately, Beate's parents Leo and Augustine survived the bombing; they had been previously ordered by authorities to move to an internment camp in Karuizawa, more than one hundred miles north of Tokyo. Like the Sirotas, most foreigners in Japan had been relocated to the summer resort of Karuizawa—ostensibly for their own protection from the bombings (and possible retaliation)—most certainly because a single location made them easier to control and ensured that they could not communicate with enemy forces.

Like many expatriates in Tokyo, the Sirota family had been accustomed to escaping from many hot and unbearably humid Tokyo summers to the small mountain resort of Karuizawa. Their "cottage" was nestled amidst birch forests, and the couple had once cherished the pleasures of their extended social life there in the company of affluent and westernized Japanese friends. But the very fact that Karuizawa was small and self-contained convinced Japanese authorities that it would be the most convenient location to hold foreigners and keep them under close watch.

However, the resort was not meant for the winter months. Most of the summer cottages had no insulation or central heating, and fuel was scarce. Located on an open plateau battered by harsh winds, Karuizawa's temperatures fell below freezing for several months each winter. During their internment, Leo and Augustine suffered from both intense cold and intense hunger. Food rations authorized by Japanese authorities were notoriously small, forcing the Sirotas to obtain additional food through the black market from farmers who often insisted on being paid not with cash but with clothes or other goods. When Leo was not practicing his music (he and Augustine had both brought their pianos, and Leo played three hours daily), he was scouring the countryside in search of food, and the forests in search of wood to burn. He was banned from teaching music to Japanese citizens. Nevertheless, some of his students traveled in secret from Tokyo to continue their training. And, following an eruption of nearby Mount

Asama, one student even managed to smuggle a large piece of glass to Leo to replace the smashed windows of his cottage and keep out the freezing winds.

More than the hunger or the cold, however, it was fear that most tormented the foreign residents of Karuizawa. The Japanese military police were omnipresent, and their interrogations could be relentless. Arrests were so feared that one foreign resident, called in for a second round of questioning, chose instead to commit suicide. The foreign community was constantly subject to rumors and panic. After the fall of Okinawa, foreigners in Japan became convinced they would all be exterminated out of revenge if the Americans invaded Japan—which had indeed been planned, before the decision to drop the atomic bombs was made.

On July 31, 1945, the military police abruptly appeared at the Sirota home; the couple was particularly suspect due to the fact that their daughter was living in the United States, an enemy territory. Leo received instructions to report to the police within one week. He remained convinced until the end of his life that, had the war lasted another few weeks, he would not have survived.

At the end of the war, in the midst of the rubble, musical life returned almost immediately—a ray of hope for a devastated nation. Leo gave his first post-war concert on 16 November 1945, under the direction of Rosenstock. Rosenstock, too, had been exiled to Karuizawa, but after the war he was immediately reinstated into his post at the head of the Radio Orchestra. Leo, on the other hand, remained uncertain about his future. The Americans had installed a new government, and their Ministry of Education offered him his old teaching post at the Academy of Music. But Leo was soon embroiled in internal strife among the faculty, and ultimately felt obligated to refuse (his students had the feeling that he had been outright dismissed). Finally, in May 1946, Leo and Augustine relocated to the United States and left Japan for good.

At sixty years old, Leo was bitter that he had wasted an international career, experienced cold, hunger, fear, and ultimately ingratitude from a country to which he had given so much—using all his energy to build the foundations of the country's school of piano. But he also owed it to Japan to have survived. His brother Pierre, the Parisian impresario, was not as fortunate. Having joined the Resistance in France, Pierre was arrested by the Gestapo in February 1944 while in hiding in the French Department of the Isère. He was transferred through Drancy and murdered in Auschwitz.

Augustine

The following is a typed text discovered in the rich archives Beate kept on the activities of her parents. It appears to be the draft of an autobiography that Leo's wife, Augustine, probably intended to write about the World War II years.

Chapter I: September 1941

I BEGIN MY STORY BY SAYING that I am the wife of the pianist Leo Sirota, the head of the piano department of the Imperial Academy of Music in Tokyo, Japan. I am awaiting him anxiously in a hotel in San Francisco, eager to know what impressions he will bring back from Los Angeles, where he went to see immigrant musician friends from Europe who are trying to get settled in the US. I know that his talks with them will be crucial in the decision we will make about staying in the US or going back to Japan to fulfill his contract with the

Imperial Academy. We had come to the States on the *Tatsuta Maru*, the ship which made history, because it was the last ship to bring silk to the US before the war, and for six days it drifted in the international waters off San Francisco while US authorities tried to decide whether or not to let it dock. It was only during those six days that we realized how serious the political situation between the US and Japan had become. We began to think that although we had come to the US only with the idea of seeing our daughter, Beate, attending college in Oakland, California, we should start seriously thinking about moving to the US. Leo comes back from Los Angeles depressed, can't see a future for himself in US, insists on returning to Japan, saying that in spite of everything, he doesn't think war will break out. I want to stay. We have bitter discussions. He wins out. We have difficulties getting ship reservations— very few ships are going to Japan and most are fully booked. Finally arrangements are made, and we leave for Honolulu on our way back to Japan. We say good- bye to our daughter. Upon arrival in Honolulu, American immigration officials tell us we can't get an exit permit unless we get FBI clearance papers. These are necessary because although we are Austrians, we carry German passports—the aftermath of the Anschluss. Frantic telegrams to Washington and our old friend

Ambassador [Joseph] Grew in Tokyo, asking for speedy arrangements of these matters. My husband worries about getting back to Japan in time for the beginning of the academic year. Nevertheless, while waiting for an answer, we have a marvelous time in Honolulu, my husband gives concerts, there are lavish parties, we see old friends, etc. Papers are finally put in order, and we leave on the twelfth of November, on the last ship to leave US territory for Japan. Newspapers and friends see us off—it is a sad good-bye.

Chapter II: November 18, 1941
WE ARRIVE IN JAPAN. OUR JAPANESE lawyer meets us at the boat to warn us that we are under suspicion of spying. The reason for Secret Police suspicion: when leaving for our vacation in the US, our friend, the representative of the Czech Government[1], came to see us off at the ship and handed me an envelope to be mailed in the US, which unbeknownst to me, contained letters addressed to [Jan] Masaryk and [Edvard] Beneš. Our lawyer says we must be careful when questioned by the Police. We go to our home, where our cook also tells us that we must be careful, because the

---

1 F. Havlicek was the former Czech envoy to Japan. By March 1939, the Japanese government had broken off diplomatic ties with Czechoslovakia, no longer recognizing it as a sovereign nation. Havlicek was obviously seeking to send a letter to Beneš and Masaryk, president and foreign minister respectively, of the provisional Czech government-in-exile, based in London.

secret police have come to question her. The next
day our pictures are in the papers, as the only two
foreigners having arrived on the last ship from
Honolulu. We take up our routine, my husband
teaches at the Imperial Academy every day, there is
an air of anxiety and insecurity in Tokyo, our friends
think we are mad to have returned at this time since
German Nazi influence has become more and more
apparent in Japan. They tell us that the passports of
all foreigners are being checked by the Japanese
authorities. True enough, the Japanese secret police
come to question us about our trip to the US and
especially about our friend, the Czech diplomat, who
they tell us has been arrested and put in prison on
suspicion of spying. However they do not threaten
us with anything and leave. My husband goes to
see Ambassador Grew to thank him for his help
with straightening out the papers. The Ambassador
expresses his hope that the current tension between
Japan and US will ease. My husband has an appointment with the head of the Imperial Academy, a
retired Army general, who welcomes him back and
assures him that German influence will not make
him change the personnel of the Academy on the
basis of people being Aryans or non-Aryans. After
these interviews, Leo is happy and confident that he

made the right decision. On December sixth, my husband goes to Osaka to teach a master class. He comes back December seventh to Tokyo—he hasn't read the papers or listened to the radio. When he comes home, he finds me in a state of distraction and for the first time hears that Pearl Harbor has been bombed.

Chapter 3: 1941–1943

As the first few months of the war pass, life begins to change in Tokyo. The city is crowded with military personnel, military bands play all over the city, soldiers departing for the front are being seen off by hundreds of women with babies strapped to their backs. On the streets, women approach you and ask you to sew a stitch in a cloth belt which will then be given to a soldier as a good luck omen, to keep the bullets away. And soon, small wooden boxes wrapped in white cloth and filled with the ashes of soldiers, are being carried in processions from the military barracks. The aspect of the city itself changes also. There are fewer taxis on the streets, grocery stores which formerly had been filled with goods increasingly show empty shelves. Soap and chocolate become scarce. Our life goes on, superficially with the same routine—Leo teaching and concertizing, etc.— except for a visit three times a week by the secret police, always asking the same questions. Do you have a shortwave radio? Whom do you want to win the war? etc., etc. I burn all private letters which I think may be misunderstood if found by the police. Although my husband and I are non-political people, I am afraid that letters written in foreign languages might make for trouble. During this time also, I have the doubtful pleasure of becoming the teacher of a secret policeman who wants to pass an exam in the Russian language. By mistake he leaves very interesting Russian radio reports on my desk, which give me some insight into what is happening in the outside world, since all we read and hear is censored. Many rumors are circulated among the foreigners, usually picked up at bridge parties held at the European doctor's house. He has a fund of information because among his patients are diplomats of neutral and Axis countries who speak freely to him. Some of them have shortwave radios, and through the grapevine, we hear about the losses and successes of the Allies. Many Americans who are afraid of being arrested flee to the compound of the American Embassy which has diplomatic immunity. By the time summer comes along, we go up to Karuizawa, in the mountains, as we had done for many years—little did we know then that soon we would be there not by volition but by force, required to spend three miserable winters there in fear, hunger, and desperation. After the summer we return to Tokyo.

Economic conditions have become worse. The German Embassy is actively trying to eliminate non-Aryan teachers from Japanese institutions. Articles appear in German papers denouncing by name Leo and others, but especially Leo as having brought in many non-Aryans. Leo starts worrying about his position at the Academy, and by the end of the year, he is called in by the head of the Academy, and told that he no longer can teach there. Soon thereafter he is prohibited from playing on the radio or with orchestras. He makes his livelihood by teaching privately. The situation in Tokyo is becoming worse. Air raid drills are being held constantly and many Europeans are starting to build air raid shelters. We, too, build one. Our cook, who has been with us for ten years, starts to complain that she cannot get enough food for the children in Tokyo and wants to return to her parents in the country. I tell her to go since I cannot take the responsibility of providing for her children. We witness the Doolittle Raid[2]—as seen from our garden. After the raid, we are told we must leave Tokyo and go to live in

---

2 The Doolittle Raid, named after James "Jimmy" Doolittle, the US Air Force lieutenant colonel who led the attack, was the first successful air raid of Japanese territory by American aviation, flying off an aircraft carrier some 1,000 kilometers from the coasts. The famously audacious attack took place in April 1942. It was meant to demonstrate to the Japanese that their archipelago was far from invulnerable. It seems, therefore, that Augustine may be confusing this attack with air raids that took place in autumn 1944, after the American victory at the battle of Saipan (*See* p. 24–25), and which was to lead the Japanese government to move foreign residents of Tokyo to Karuizawa.

Karuizawa where all foreigners will live together. Waiting for days in Tokyo, for the truck to take our belongings to the mountains.

Chapter 4

LIFE IN KARUIZAWA—MOVING INTO A SMALL summer house which is to be our home for the next three years— no one to help us. What a difference compared to the time when I first arrived in Japan and moved from the Imperial Hotel into our first house—we had had fifteen delivery boys helping us under the direction of our cook, who wouldn't give them food orders until they had put the whole house in order. What a difference, too, in maids. The one here in Karuizawa, unhappy about working for an "enemy," reporting to the Secret Police daily about our activities, etc.

Our life is quite different now. Food is rationed, Leo is prohibited from teaching Japanese pupils, and I take over making a living. I get students from the various foreign embassies who are all living in Karuizawa. Leo spends most of his time riding his bicycle, looking for food. He buys food on the black market—the farmers won't sell only for money, they want goods, too. But the Nazis are the ones who have many goods to be bartered because they have the loot plundered by the Germans from Australian ships. This makes it difficult for other foreigners to barter things which are not as new as the ones offered by the Nazis.

On the main street of Karuizawa people are afraid to talk to each other when there are more than three in a group. As the bombings of Tokyo increase, the secret police increase their visits to Karuizawa's foreign population. One or two foreigners are arrested. But it is still spring and summer, and life is tolerable until the winter. The houses are summer houses, and have only one pot-bellied stove on each floor. Fuel is scarce and expensive. We trade shoes and men's suits for fuel. Trying to get the stoves started in below zero weather makes me cry many times. We walk around the house in fur coats and boots in the early mornings and evenings. The only time it is warm in the house is from noon until four, while the sun in shining. The water pipes often burst in the kitchen overnight, and in the morning the kitchen floor is like an ice skating rink. Bridge parties are held in whoever's house has enough fuel to warm the living room for an evening. The New Year's party is held in the house of a former department store buyer, and everyone knows weeks in advance that the surprise will be a hot bath for all the guests, in Japanese fashion, of course, that is, the same bath water for everyone. I, as the guest of honor, am the first to enter the bath, and while luxuriating in this uncommon pleasure, I remember when my husband first learned about a Japanese bath, when he was invited by a gentleman, sitting in a bath with two ladies, who said "Do step in, this is only my wife and my daughter."

Foraging for food is the most important daily activity. The diplomats have good rations, as much as one pound of butter a day, while our rations are meager. The diplomats hoard, afraid that their rations will be cut later on, and do not give anything to the other foreigners. Among ourselves, we divide with each other whatever we can buy on the black market, but the sellers cheat us in weight, etc. Sometimes, during the night, a Japanese friend leaves a basket of food on the front porch anonymously—we hear the cat meowing, smelling the package, and rush out to see what it is. Daily life includes such calamities as Mount Asama[3] erupting (at first we think it's an air raid), and all the windows breaking in the house. Glass not replaceable. Finally a former student from Tokyo brings the glass carrying it on her back—a 120-mile train trip.

Some students, although forbidden to communicate with Leo, do come from Tokyo, to take lessons from him secretly. One of the students gets arrested and put in jail for a week for having told the police that Leo should get special rations for all he has done for the Japanese.

---

3 A highly active volcano dominating the Karuizawa plateau, and which was in eruption for long periods of time in 1944 and 1945.

Rumors of more people getting arrested. One of them who gets released is so afraid of another arrest, that he takes his own life. All foreigners start to fear for themselves. Our former German friends try not to recognize us on the streets, but one of them brings us a bag of rice at night. Friendships break up because of disputes about three pounds of meat and two pounds of rice. When a diplomat's child makes particular progress in piano, I receive a pound of butter or a package of cigarettes. In general, each nationality group keeps to itself as much as possible, interested only in its own survival.

We try to add to our food supply by buying two live chickens. Our neighbor complains about the chickens eating their plants. The chickens become our egg suppliers, and one day a chicken flies up into a tree and can't get down. I make a secret policeman get it down.

The summer comes. We are thankful for the warmth. I begin to write about my life—how I got to Japan, and what it was like before this terrible war.

Legacy Part I: Article 24

ON NOVEMBER 3, 1946 THE JAPANESE Diet approved a constitution which was to usher in a new era for an ancient but utterly defeated and destitute nation. After fifteen years of a war that had ended in the nuclear catastrophes of Hiroshima and Nagasaki, millions of Japanese were to invest in this new document their aspirations for a better life and a different future. In so doing, they defied their leaders and other naysayers, who considered the constitution too liberal and not Japanese enough; they also ignored the open rumors that (rightly) attributed the constitution's original drafting to the American Occupation. The most revolutionary of the one hundred and three articles—known today around the world as the "Peace Constitution"—was Article 9, which forever renounced "war as a sovereign right of the nation and the threat or use of force as means of settling international disputes." But another, smaller revolution was in the making with a different paragraph: Article 24, which gave Japanese women some of the most far-reaching equal rights of the time.

Article 24 reads as follows:

> Marriage shall be based only on the mutual consent of both sexes and it shall be maintained through mutual cooperation with the equal rights of husband and wife as a basis. With regard to choice of spouse, property rights, inheritance, choice of domicile, divorce, and other matters pertaining to marriage and the family, laws shall be enacted from the standpoint of individual dignity and essential equality of the sexes.

Never before had the legal document of the land so clearly spelled out the equal rights of half of the country's population, from the first Japanese constitution—a seventeen-article document drafted in 604 AD by Prince Shôtoku—through the Meiji Constitution of 1889. And for the following forty years, the person responsible for developing this revolutionary article remained a secret. Few could imagine that the women's rights article in the new constitution of Japan was the work of a then twenty-two-year-old European-born American of Ukrainian descent who had grown up in Japan. Her name was Beate Sirota and her legacy remains to this day. Though much of her original draft was edited or outright discarded, its core ambition—ensuring the equal rights of Japanese women—has thus far remained firmly in place.

IT IS HARD TO IMAGINE A more promising start to life than that of Beate. She was born on October 25, 1923 in Vienna, to Augustine (Horenstein) and Leo Sirota. Since her earliest days Beate remembers a household both warm and refined, of two socially active, outgoing, and artistic parents, secular Jews who from an early age would imbue her with their universalist, humanistic values.

Beate's lifelong connection to Japan began in 1929. That year, the small family had packed their belongings, entrusted their Vienna apartment to the hands of an agent, and left for Japan, traveling thirteen days via the Trans-Siberian railway to Vladivostok, and then on to Yokohama by ferry. Leo and Augustine had set out to stay in Japan for only six months, but it would be more than sixteen years before they would leave for good. As for Beate, she would spend the next ten formative years of her life in Japan.

Undoubtedly, all this travel and upheaval must have been quite an adventure for a naturally fearless child of five and a half. Beate seemed to take to her new country like a fish to water. She was soon out and about, making friends and finding playmates among the children of her upper middle class neighborhood. The product of a cosmopolitan culture and household where German, Russian, French, and English were spoken, she remembers having begun to speak Japanese within three months of arrival—in part, prompted by necessity. She quickly became her parents' de facto interpreter.

Life in Tokyo was busy. In addition to classes at the German school, there were piano and dance lessons, and an endless number of concerts and performances. The Sirota couple went everywhere—Kabuki, Noh, concerts—and often took Beate with them. Luckily for Leo, Japan in those years was deep in the throes of passion for all things Western, and audiences could not get enough of his performances. He gave concerts around the country, frequently accompanied by his wife and daughter. In addition to his ever-increasing number of private students, Leo also began teaching at the Imperial Academy of Music, and the Sirota home gradually became a cultural salon frequented by foreign and Japanese artists alike, who gathered there as much for the music and the conversation as for the delicious meals hosted by Augustine.

Indeed, life in the early thirties was fulfilling for the Sirota family. But Japan's democratic aspirations, which had begun with the Meiji Restoration of 1868, were fast eroding. Beate's idyllic youth was soon to be replaced with the harsh realities of prejudice, threats of violence and the brutal devastation of war. To better understand the underlying forces behind the dramatic changes in Japanese society, and how they affected Beate's life, it is useful to become familiar with a brief overview of a succession of political events leading up to the second world war.

FROM 1868 THROUGH 1912, THE MEIJI era successfully opened Japan to the West after an isolationist period of almost two hundred and fifty years under the Tokugawa Shogunate. Reforms soon paved the way to increased wealth and prosperity. The achievements of this modernization period surely rank as one of the most radical transformations of any feudal society.

The road to the Meiji era began with the arrival of American Commodore Matthew C. Perry's black ships near Tokyo Bay in 1853. Japanese leaders quickly grasped the consequences of their country's technological inferiority and became eager to catch up with Western powers, in part, to diminish the possibility of colonization. The country soon plunged into an era of modernization with a fervor and a national cohesion rarely matched in history. From infrastructure development, transportation, education, health, and architecture, to music, painting, and literary production—all elements of society changed with lightning speed in the new era, leaving no aspect of life unaffected.

For most of the late nineteenth century, Germany served as one of the Meiji government's closest partners. Many of the newly acquired social mores of the Japanese ruling classes (and indeed its entire educational system) were based on Bismarck's Germany. In most disciplines—from engineering to medicine, law, governance, and infrastructure development—Germany was the teacher, Japan the student. The Meiji Constitution itself, promulgated in February 1889, was extensively inspired by (some even say copied from) its German homologue, which numerous Japanese scholars and indeed entire visiting delegations had studied for a number of years. If the relationship was not particularly affectionate, it was nonetheless most productive and remained intense until the turn of the century. However, during World War I, Japan sided with Britain against Germany.

During the 1920s, Japanese zeal for Westernization began to diminish. Prompted by fears of Western imperial powers and their lust for Asia's resources, and shaken by the consequences of the hostile US Immigration Act of 1924 and the market crash of 1929, Japan took a turn to the right. The nascent foundations developed by the liberal Taishō Democracy following World War I were gradually dismantled. An increasingly militaristic ruling establishment sealed its power with the Manchurian Incident of 1931, Japan's withdrawal from the League of Nations in 1933, and finally the full-scale invasion of China in 1937.

The rise of Hitler and the National Socialists in Germany in the early thirties coincided with Japan's militarization, and ties were soon renewed between the two anti-democratic governments. At the time, Joseph Goebbels, the Reich Minister of Public Enlightenment and Propaganda, was pushing for a policy of "Nazification" of German schools around the world, and the German school in Tokyo, where Beate was enrolled, soon adhered to the party line. By 1935, most of its teachers had been replaced by Nazi sympathizers. In 1936, when animosity toward Beate's Jewishness—especially among the teachers—became intolerable, her parents moved her to the American school in Tokyo. The American educational system was more lax than what she had known until then, and at first Beate felt the change as something of a demotion. But she soon adapted to the more informal and creative atmosphere of American education—and indeed came to find it a breath of fresh air after the rigidity and constraints of the German system.

Meanwhile, the general situation for many foreigners was growing increasingly tense. The German embassy in Tokyo actively sought to turn public opinion against artists of Jewish descent, many of whom had fled Europe and were living and teaching in Japan at the time. Its shrill anti-Semitic campaigns were not particularly effective however, partly because so many of the best-loved Western artists and teachers of upper class Japanese children were European Jews. In addition, the continued support of Western cultural figures reflected long-held sentiments of the Japanese, who were, in general, less prejudiced about differences of faith.

In 1939, not yet sixteen, Beate graduated from the American school, and the inevitable question arose of where she would undertake her college education (it was of course a given, in the enlightened Sirota household, that she would receive a college education). Increasingly, war-obsessed Japan could no longer be a serious consideration. In fact, with the expanding front in China and the country's swelling hostility toward most foreigners, it seemed urgent that Beate leave as soon as possible. Her first choice for college had been the Sorbonne in Paris. But the situation in Europe, especially for Jews, was also worsening daily, making enrolling there a risky prospect. Concerned for her safety, Beate and her family decided she would instead attend Mills College, a respected all-women liberal arts college near San Francisco.

In early August 1939, Beate, accompanied by her parents, sailed on a San Francisco-bound freighter from Yokohama Port, arriving eleven days later. Within a few weeks, Leo and Augustine returned to Japan, and Beate found herself living alone for the first time in her life.

BEATE RETURNED TO TOKYO FOR THE summer holidays in May, 1940. The din of war had become even louder and the military's influence on politics and almost all other aspects of daily life the norm. As usual, the Sirota family spent the summer at their cottage in the Japanese mountain resort, Karuizawa, but the ooverall atmosphere in the nation was bleak and many foreigners had begun to leave. At the end of the summer, Beate returned to San Francisco, but this time her parents stayed behind.

She would see her parents only once more before the start of war, in July 1941, when Leo and Augustine visited San Francisco. Throughout their stay, the key preoccupation was whether they should remain in America, or return to Japan. Augustine wanted to stay, Leo to return. He felt Japan still offered the best opportunities for him as a musician and a teacher. And he had already accomplished so much there. He trusted Japan, and he trusted the future. He was to be proven wrong on both counts. When he and Augustine sailed to Hawaii, and from there boarded the last boat to Yokohama in late November 1941, they did not know that within a few days, Japan would bomb Pearl Harbor, sparking the Pacific War. It would be four long, anguish-filled years before Beate would see her parents again.

THOSE WHO MET BEATE IN LATER life could hardly imagine the kind of disciplined student and driven professional she had been, given her exuberance, humor, warm informality, and lighthearted stories of her privileged childhood. At Mills, she earned a scholarship, and from 1942 onward, when money from home was frozen, she held a job in addition to her full class load.

Beate was particularly well-suited for work as a translator. Her mastery of six languages—and of Japanese in particular—was a tremendous asset during those dark times when Japanese-American citizens were being persecuted and interned en masse, and Caucasian speakers of Japanese were few and far between. While still in college, she worked as a linguist at CBS Radio Broadcasting in San Francisco. When she graduated in 1943, she already had a full-fledged career with the Japanese programs of the Foreign

Broadcasting Intelligence Service (FBIS) and there-after with the Office of War Information (OWI). Barely twenty, just out of college, she was not only translating but also writing and delivering programs for broadcast into Japan.

In March 1945, as the bloody final months of the war came to a close, Beate moved to New York City for an assignment as a foreign affairs researcher with *TIME* magazine. It was heady stuff for such a young woman. Decades later, she still sounded enchanted with both the job and with New York City, which in a few years would become "her" city. In those days, *TIME* employed women only as research assistants (there were still no female reporters), yet Beate's experience as a foreign affairs researcher was nonetheless transfor-mative. She found herself in good company, mentored by politically engaged and learned, older European women, two of whom she shared a basement apartment with in New York. In the magazine's high-pressure environment, Beate improved her research skills. In the temperamentally calm and measured Beate, New York would forge a more politically engaged personality.

Since her parents' departure from San Francisco in November of 1941, Beate had heard very little from them. In fact, in Japan, Leo and Augustine had been forcibly moved from the home Beate had grown up in and were forbidden to write letters to their daughter in the enemy country of America. During the war years, Beate had no idea of their struggles with agonizing cold and scarcity of food. As the bombing of Japanese cities intensified in the final months of the war, the treatment of foreigners became even more dire, and even the well-connected Beate had a hard time getting information from inside the country. Only sporadic news of her parents trickled out, and none of it directly from them.

On August 15, 1945, the Emperor of Japan announced his country's surrender to the Allies, and the Pacific War—which had caused the death of some thirty-six million human beings—ended at last. That October, Beate received news from a *TIME* reporter inside Japan that her parents were alive and in Karuizawa, and so the war finally came to a close for her, too. Due to travel restrictions, she knew she could not get back to Japan as a private citizen, so the resourceful twenty-two-year-old applied for a position with the Foreign Economic Administration, which at the time was looking to staff the Occupation. Thanks to her fluent Japanese and superb research skills, Beate quickly got the job, becoming the first civilian woman to join General MacArthur's staff in the early months of the Occupation.

In December 1945, Beate flew into the Atsugi air base, then made her way to a scorched and unrecognizable Tokyo. She detailed that experience in the opening pages of her autobiography *The Only Woman in the Room*, giving the reader a real sense of the shock and anxiety she felt—rare for a woman who, in her memoir, as in life, rarely dwelt on personal emotions.

But at least her parents were alive. After an emotional reunion, Beate's practical instincts resurfaced. In quick succession she found food to barter, as well as housing and medical care for Leo and Augustine—scarce commodities even for the victors in those days of ruined cities and famine—and in May of 1946 saw them off to America. For the next seventeen years, her father refused to return to the country he had once so loved. In 1964, he finally accepted a concert tour organized by three hundred of his former students in what proved to be an intense and emotional final reconciliation just a few months before his death. Despite being so badly treated by the Japanese authorities throughout the war years, Beate recalled that her father had confided only to feeling "offended." Hatred had never been in Leo's lexicon—a quality his daughter had clearly inherited.

After sending her parents to America, Beate remained in Japan, continuing to work at the General Headquarters of the Supreme Commander for the Allied

Powers (SCAP)—in reality, an entirely American Occupation. She was assigned to the Government Section and even though day-to-day life remained difficult, even for extremely privileged Americans, the work provided her with great intellectual and personal satisfaction.

THE CHALLENGES OF THE OCCUPATION—AS MUCH for the vanquished as for the victor—must have been daunting. The objective was nothing less than the total reform of a country which for the previous four years had been the bitterest of foes. The success of the operation may also be attributed to thorough preparation by the Americans for post-war occupation, made during the war, demonstrating foresight—and, perhaps, elevated self-confidence. As detailed in *Japan Transformed*, "During World War II, the Roosevelt administration assembled an all-star group of bureaucrats and academic consultants to address the question of what went wrong in Japan, in anticipation of the day when victorious Allied forces would occupy Japan and prepare it for the reemergence in world affairs as a peace-loving nation."[1] This careful planning was to expand even more in the later stages of the war, as Shoichi Koseki, a professor of law at Dokkyo University, describes:

1 *Japan Transformed*, Frances McCall Rosenbluth and Michael F. Thies, Princeton University Press, 2010, p 43.

The US Civil Affairs Division set up Civil Affairs Training Schools (CATS) at Harvard, Yale, Chicago, Stanford, Michigan, and Northwestern universities in the summer of 1944, one year before Japan was defeated. Under teachers who had studied in Japanese universities before the war, the students took intensive courses, in the Japanese language, in Japanese economy, local government and educational system. Fifteen hundred civil administrators were believed necessary in the occupation of Japan. The training was very rigorous and the classes in Japanese lasted five hours a day.[2]

It also helped that General Douglas MacArthur, head of SCAP, was among the United States military's more knowledgeable officers on Asia. His early assignments had led him to the Philippines, where his father had been military Governor-General (and where he later became an influential military advisor in 1937). Between 1904 and 1905, as a young lieutenant, he had accompanied his father on a ten-month tour of Asia. His familiarity with both Japan and China and his ability to use that insight, his affinity for pomp and brinkmanship, coupled with his intuitive grasp of the psychology of the Japanese following their defeat— exhausted and humiliated by the losses of war and the continued deprivations of peace—informed his rule, making it particularly effective. While not universally liked, he was broadly respected, especially by the

---

2 "An historical perspective of post-war Japan," in *Post-Conflict Reconstruction...*, *op. cit.*, pp. 51-60.

ordinary Japanese. By her own account, young Beate was so in awe of MacArthur that she would hide behind a pillar every time she saw him in the lobby of the Dai-Ichi Hotel, the headquarters of SCAP.

Especially in the early years of the Occupation, the Government Section was staffed by many well-educated, idealistic liberals—a generation influenced by Roosevelt's New Deal-era policies and philosophy.[3] Beate had the good fortune to work under the direct supervision of the deputy chief of section—an intelligent, able and charismatic lawyer named Charles Kades. Also of European descent, Kades was to have a strong influence on ensuring the passage of some of the civil rights laws of the new constitution.

By the time Beate arrived in December 1945, the Americans and the Japanese government were already in disagreement over how the new constitution should be drafted. The Americans believed the Meiji Constitution had encouraged Japan's militarization and were adamant that it be replaced. However, many Japanese officials challenged that belief, contending instead that minor amendments to the existing constitution should be more than

---

3 By 1947, fear of the Soviets and the start of the Cold War, alongside rising McCarthyism in the US, brought about what is known as the "Reverse Course" in US policies vis-à-vis Japan, in an attempt to use that nation as a buffer against communism. Many of the idealistic members of the Occupation were sidetracked after this period; however the policies they had formulated could not be entirely dismantled.

sufficient. A first attempt, prepared by former prime minister Prince Fumimaro Konoe, had been outright ignored (later Konoe, upon learning that he had been identified as a Class-A criminal, would commit suicide). The Japanese government then formed a committee of scholars—headed by the legal expert and minister of state Joji Matsumoto—which spent almost six months essentially tinkering with the existing constitution. That version, too, was deemed unacceptable—and not only by the Americans, but by many Japanese (its contents had been leaked to the press, and it was quickly ridiculed by much of the media for its conservative positions). For people who knew Japan intimately like Beate did, it was clear that ordinary, everyday people—even as they were struggling for survival—were more willing than the political and academic elite to discard the Meiji Constitution and start afresh.

As for General MacArthur, a new Japanese constitution was to be his legacy, the instrument of Japan's transformation into a democratic society. On this point, at least, he worked from a position of principle. And certainly there were other, more pragmatic, considerations: with the establishment of the Far Eastern Commission (FEC), and increasing external and internal pressures to indict the Emperor for war crimes, there was a real sense that the window of opportunity was closing fast. The stakes were rising. A rapid and timely constitutional revision could ensure the survival of the imperial household. MacArthur was not alone in this feeling; many in the imperial palace shared his view. Frustrated by the Matsumoto debacle, MacArthur decided that a team at SCAP's own Government Section should work on a new draft and informed its head, his own close advisor General Courtney Whitney, that the team had *nine* days—until February 12, 1946—to complete the task.

Under the leadership of deputy chief of section Kades, a "constitutional convention" of sorts was set up and various committees formed. Beate was assigned to the committee examining civil rights and those feverish days would soon become one of the most intellectually challenging periods of her life. For her colleagues—sworn to secrecy about the special assignment and therefore limited in their ability to involve other Japanese researchers—Beate's familiarity with pre-war Tokyo, her mastery of Japanese, and her research skills proved invaluable. She promptly mobilized a Jeep and a driver, and drove to all the libraries still standing in war-torn Tokyo. By her own account, she found about a dozen different constitutions, from Denmark (1881 and 1882 versions), Sweden (1809), Finland (1919), the Weimar Republic (1919), Portugal (1935), Austria (1861), Ireland (1937), Uruguay (1918), Belgium (1831), Switzerland (1848), and, of course, the

Constitution and the Declaration of Independence of the United States of America. However, Beate was careful not to collect all these documents from a single library— SCAP was particularly wary of starting rumors about the new constitution.

As a framework, the team relied on the three prerequisites known as the MacArthur Notes: the safeguard of a dynastic but symbolic emperor representative of the people; the renunciation of war; and the dismantling of the feudal system. Thus, they started by completely discarding the Meiji document, including the Konoe and Matsumoto revisions. Though in this sense they may have begun tabula rasa, there was to be much Japanese input. Indeed some twelve different versions had been submitted to SCAP by a broad variety of interested parties other than the government—from the socialists and the communists to a public association set up for constitutional research by prominent intellectuals.

The drafters[4] worked nonstop and though General MacArthur followed their progress closely, he did not intervene. Astonishingly, this allowed for some of his own conservative leanings to be overridden by more liberal-minded members, Kades in particular. Beate was assigned to work on the women's rights clause (she also

---

4 Almost all of the Government Section was part of the drafting team, which consisted of a steering committee overseeing seven others, including the civil rights committee of which Beate was a member.

requested she be assigned to draft the clause on academic freedoms). Had her original versions been kept, the constitution would surely have had the most advanced equal rights clauses of any country. But she did not entirely prevail; her text was cut substantially by the steering committee during the final, heated editing session on February 12, and many of her beloved civil rights inclusions were removed from the final version.[5] MacArthur approved the new draft, after which it was briskly delivered to the Japanese foreign minister and his aides. On February 22, a tearful cabinet agreed, in principle, to enter negotiations with SCAP based on the new text. On March 4, Beate, one of the fastest interpreters at the Government Section, attended the negotiations as translator (she was the only female staff present, which prompted the title of her autobiography *The Only Woman in the Room*), joining in a thirty-six-hour marathon round of impassioned debates and translation efforts. Disagreements, both on substantive issues and terminology, were huge. The interpretation pool on the American side, headed by Lt. Joseph Gordon, Beate's future husband, had its hands full as it struggled

---

5 Beate had included in her drafts provisions as extensive as the rights of expecting and nursing mothers and full medical, dental, and optical treatment for school-age children. The steering committee had argued that such details would have to be worked out in the civil code of the country once the constitution had been adopted, and overrode Beate's concerns that the conservative bureaucracy could not be trusted to include such progressive rights when it came to drafting the laws. Sadly, she was proven right over the years.

to ensure identical meaning between the English and Japanese versions.[6]

Throughout the negotiations Beate's language abilities and natural affinity with the Japanese side had been noted and appreciated. It was fortuitous, that when the women's rights article came under heavy criticism by the Japanese negotiators in the middle of the night, Kades—whether out of conviction or sheer exhaustion one shall never know—made a plea to the Japanese side to agree to its passage, for the sake of "Miss Sirota." They accepted.

The completion of a new constitution approved by the Japanese cabinet, the emperor, and the privy council was announced on March 6, and Beate, who sat in the Diet chamber for the announcement, later recalled most vividly the newspaper headlines: "New Constitution Draft Rejects War."[7] The constitution was promulgated on November 3, 1946 and became the law of the land six months later.

To this day, and with varying degrees of ebb and flow, the debate continues about whether or not the constitution of Japan is really Japanese. Frequently the issue is seized by conservatives or right wing politicians, who

---

6 Thanks to his phenomenal photographic memory Joe would still recall, well into his nineties, the details of most of the substantive changes made in the Japanese translation of the draft constitution.

7 *The Only Woman in the Room—A Memoir*, Kodansha International, 1997 (reprint, University of Chicago Press, 2014), p. 124.

claim that it should be scrapped and rewritten, in toto, to reflect "real" Japanese values and traditions. Just as frequently, those who have directly benefited from it—women at the forefront—have put up a fight to protect "their" document. Due to the fear of the unknown, that even a minor change may open a Pandora's box of complexities, the constitution has remained immovable, quasi unchanged sixty-seven years after its adoption. Indeed, it is by now one of the oldest constitutions in the world.

The controversy and debates may well never end. One essential aspect of the Japanese constitution, at times overlooked in the emotional analyses of its "authenticity," is that while it was clearly a text drafted by the SCAP team, the Japanese input was not negligible. As mentioned earlier, other than the Konoe and Matsumoto versions, a number of other drafts had been submitted to SCAP—including versions by the Socialist Party and the *Kempō Kenkyūkai* (Research Committee for the Constitution). It had then been negotiated and discussed by the Diet throughout the adoption process (some of the more liberal elements in SCAP actually encouraged an even greater involvement by the legislature). At any rate, as Beate and others have often argued, the text was not entirely an "American text"—but one that was inspired and influenced to a large extent by different constitutions of the nineteenth and twentieth centuries.

At its core, it is imbued with universal principles of human rights and democracy, something most of the American side—and Beate most certainly—believed to be the desire of the Japanese people as well.

ONCE THE VEIL OF SECRECY WAS lifted on Beate's participation in drafting the constitution[8], Japanese women, young and old, immediately expressed immense adoration for her. From 1994 to 2010 when her health made it difficult to fly, Beate traveled sometimes twice a year to Japan to speak to packed houses about the women's rights clause, the constitution, and the performing arts. Quite unlike many other Western feminists whose lectures about equal rights received lukewarm responses from Japanese women, when Beate spoke about women's rights to the Japanese, she made an impact.

There may be a number of reasons for this. First, Beate's grasp of the station of women in pre-war, feudal Japan was deep and personal. True, the kind of people her parents mingled with were mostly wealthy, artistic, or scholarly. But playing out in the streets, "hanging around" with the children of the maids, and being

---

8 In fact in 1947 already, a *Christian Science Monitor* article revealed the role played by Beate in the American drafted constitution. But this news was muffled very quickly. Neither the Japanese nor the American sides—fearing a nationalistic backlash to the idea of a foreign-drafted document, especially one helped by a girl of twenty-two—wished to elaborate too much on the details. Officially, the information was made public only in the early 1970s.

observant and curious from a young age had distilled in her a genuine understanding of the place of women in Japanese society. This allowed her to speak eloquently and with visible feeling about the experience of women prior to the war. Under the Meiji constitution women had virtually no rights—no right to vote, to choose their domicile, to inherit, or to work. Beate, on the other hand, was raised in a household that, even throughout the virulent years of the rise of Nazism, communism, and many other "isms," held deep universal values of respect for the human person: male or female. Cultural diversity, artistic achievement, and personal integrity were values her parents had instilled in her from a young age, alongside a sense of her own special worth and uniqueness as a person. Beate could well see that this was not a given for countless Japanese girls.

Second, despite having finished the war on the side of the victors, and notwithstanding the mistreatment of her parents by the Japanese military police, Beate's love for Japan never wavered. She had come of age in that country, and had spent some of her happiest years there. Of course she had been nothing if not relentless in her desire to help the American victory. But her young and steely determination to do everything in her small power to help defeat Japan's aggression would never make her think of that country as "the enemy," in the easy sense. It seemed that she somehow managed, through it all, to keep in her line of vision the gap that separated ordinary people from the military rulers of Japan in the 1930s and the first half of the 1940s. That understanding never deserted her—even in later life, it remained a clear-eyed, knowing, yet unshakable attachment. For better or for worse, Japan would always remain her second home, so that when she got the chance to make a difference—in this case making life better for her Japanese friends and their mothers, daughters, wives, and sisters—and later, through her cultural work, she plunged into it wholeheartedly. She had seen too many Japanese women of all ages, from mere girls to elderly grandmothers, utterly subordinated by their men, walking behind their husbands, fathers, sons, and male in-laws. It had made her determined to change this if she could.

Furthermore, even though complaints have often been raised that the drafting of the constitution was strictly an American project, quite a few members of the drafting team at SCAP, of different national origins, did not approach their task solely as Americans. Beate was one of them. Though she had become a naturalized American citizen in January 1945 and was, in many ways, both at ease in and inspired by her new country, she was not culturally just an American—her own roots were too rich, too diverse, too deep to be easily erased. As she wrote in her memoirs and frequently stated, Beate genuinely felt that the text of the new constitution reflected the real longings and desires of ordinary Japanese, and that the diversity of sources that had informed its drafting ensured that Japan had a constitution all its own, one that was unique and benefitted from the experiences of many nations.

In 1947, after finishing her mandate with SCAP, Beate chose not to stay in Japan. By then she and Joe Gordon had decided to marry. Her parents had settled in Missouri, where Leo was teaching at the St. Louis Institute of Music, and Beate desperately wanted to be closer to them. Besides, as a young and confident woman who had glimpsed, in a few short, heady months in early 1945, the excitement and intellectual effervescence of New York, Beate was now ready to be part of that world. From then on, Japan would remain a distant home—her existence was to become solidly American. It would be years before she could return, but return she did. And once again it would be to champion the cause dearest to her heart: culture.

THE SAGA OF THE JAPANESE CONSTITUTION is ongoing. In his preface to the English Edition of *The Meiji Constitution*, the scholar Kazuhiro Takii compares the

Japanese word for constitution—*kempō*—and its connotations as a "legal document" with the English word constitution, which "contains a double sense, of both the structure and its formation or establishment. In other words, constitution seems to point to a process by which something is created and then becomes subject to ongoing analysis and verification." Any constitution, he argues, is far more than a mere legal document, but indeed the "shape of the nation . . . formed and transformed by the thoughts and hopes that people invested in it."[9]

When in 2004, the ruling Liberal Democratic Party (LDP) of Japan suggested a review of Article 24, the backlash by women's groups was immediate and massive—rallies were held across the country and Beate was frequently invited to address the crowds. When asked, in hindsight, how she felt that the Japanese Constitution, and in particular the women's rights articles, had stood the test of time, she calmly proclaimed:

> Japan is a better country today because of the freedoms enjoyed by its women, freedoms that were spelled out in the civil rights articles of the constitution. People like to constantly say that Japanese women are not equal to the men. But that is simply not true. They may not have the kinds of social freedoms enjoyed by women in some Western countries, but on just about every

---

9 *The Meiji Constitution*, International House of Japan, Tokyo, 2007, p. VII.

matter that counts—education, health, authority for child rearing, academic and professional opportunities, right to property and inheritance, decisions on marriage and divorce, and choice of domicile—they enjoy equal opportunities. In this I feel they are fully part of a worldwide trend, rightly in the vanguard.

Regarding Article 9, the "Peace Article," she was adamantly convinced that the Japanese Constitution truly reflects Japanese values, that it enshrines the best of humanity's wisdom from across the ages. Quoting the writer James Miki, Beate insisted that it was "written by the wisdom of history."

In the preface to a 2002 book on comparisons between post-conflict countries, Beate wrote:

> The basic rights of women remain, regardless of what one may say about cultural differences, one of the pillars in the rebuilding of post-war societies. Before the Second World War, Japanese women had no rights—no right to marry or divorce by choice, no right of inheritance, no right of choice of domicile or property. Today as I work with many women's groups all over Japan and see their dynamism and energy, I can but wish that donor countries would always make their reconstruction assistance conditional on women's fundamental rights being spelled out in the new constitutions of countries emerging from war and tyranny. [10]

---

10 *Post-Conflict Reconstruction . . ., op. cit.,* p. 3.

The issues Beate has raised are not merely questions of law, history, or semantics. Debates around the revision of the Japanese Constitution remain imminently political and fully current—not just in Japan, but also in Afghanistan and Iraq, and in countries now emerging from decades of one-man rule or tyranny—Egypt, Libya, Tunisia, maybe Syria, and others. What would the civil rights of women and minorities be in the new constitutions of these nations? And how will the decisions made today, about the legal framework these countries ultimately opt for, affect the life and wellbeing of their people now and for generations to come?

Beate's legacy with Article 24 raises timeless, universal questions that will surely be discussed and disputed for a long time, as well they should be.

Legacy Part II: Theaters of Asia

WHAT DOES ONE DO, HAVING BEEN at the age of twenty-two "the only woman in the room," assisting in a colossal effort to revive a country destroyed by war? In interviews, it is easy to sense how Beate Sirota Gordon's thoughts constantly pulled her back to that special time in Tokyo, in February 1946, when she became a part of history by helping draft the new constitution of Japan. However—no matter how significant—she did not allow this one single experience to remain the centerpiece of her entire existence. Upon returning to the United States, Beate worked hard to find the resources and the resilience to give new meaning and direction to the remaining decades of her life. Perhaps the greatest quality of this exceptional woman was that she knew she wanted to pursue— albeit in a different way—some of the same ideals that had led her, at such a young age, to work for justice and peace.

Though she had been immersed in music and dance since childhood, she realized early on that she was not talented enough to perform in either of these fields at a professional level. Yet, with her mastery of Japanese and her broad knowledge of the performing arts, she was uniquely suited help rekindle cultural relations between Japan and the United States.

Chance prevailed. The Japan Society, an ad hoc institution based in New York since 1907, reopened its doors in 1952 after being dormant since the attack on Pearl Harbor. Shortly thereafter, Beate was hired, initially to assist young Japanese who had come to the United States after the war to pursue their studies. Her duties included providing a general university orientation as well as handling the often precarious material conditions of these young foreigners. She was quick, though, to add a musical dimension to her work: from 1955 onward, she rented the stage at Columbia University and offered young Japanese musicians an opportunity to perform in public.

Thanks to a grant of three thousand dollars from the Japanese General Consulate in New York, Beate soon laid the foundation for a more long-term and sustainable initiative. This was essential, since the Japan

Society's primary post-war funder was John Rockefeller, III, a man so knowledgeable about Japanese art and culture that he served as cultural advisor to John Foster Dulles throughout the negotiations for the treaty of 1951, which officially ended World War II in Asia. Magnanimous though he might have been, Rockefeller's generosity was not unconditional: he demanded matching contributions. To secure the necessary funds, Beate was driven to engage the Japanese public and private sectors at a time when neither had the where-withal nor the resources to make significant financial contributions.

As the economic conditions improved, funding sources became more readily available. Beate, wishing to sensitize her students to contemporary American culture, organized an ambitious program that directly introduced them to a broad range of artists including actors Burgess Meredith and Lee Strasberg, composers Roger Sessions and John Cage, and the dancer Merce Cunningham. Most of these orientation sessions took place in an iconic location representative of contemporary architecture in New York: the modernist guest house designed by Philip Johnson for Blanchette Rockefeller—wife of the millionaire—which she used to display her modern art collection.

Beate's employers began to notice that the person they had installed as head of their educational programs possessed marked artistic tendencies herself. In 1958, when the Department for the Performing Arts of Japan Society was established, Beate was chosen as director. At the time, Beate was already part of a widespread movement—born out of the tragedy of World War II— that sought to use the performing arts to bridge cultural divides and create solidarity among different peoples. Peace, this group felt, needed to first be felt in people's hearts and minds, before it could become a formal part of international diplomacy.

In this spirit, a "Theater of Nations"—a program aimed at bringing together performing arts from all corners of the world—became the goal of the International Theatre Institute, founded in 1948 under the auspices of UNESCO. By 1957, the "Theater of Nations" became reality in Paris, following the success of the three editions of the *Festival International d'Art Dramatique de la Ville de Paris* (1954–56), which introduced the French public to a diverse mix of international artists, from poet/playwright/director Bertolt Brecht to the Peking Opera. Under the leadership of A.M. Julien of the *Théâtre Sarah Bernhardt*, and later of Jean-Louis Barrault of the *Odéon*, the Theater of Nations festival became an annual performing arts event, that flourished in Paris for more than a decade. It consolidated and united an international theatrical community, staging performances with the greatest creators of the time: Luchino Visconti, Peter Brook, Giorgio Strehler, Jerzy Grotowski, Maurice Béjart, Jerome Robbins, and more. Moreover, it presented a vast repertoire of traditional Chinese, Japanese, Indian, and African theater—in those days a rarity for the Western public.

Compared to this Parisian extravaganza, Beate's resources were extremely limited. At the time, she did not even have a dedicated performance hall for her events, which mainly included bilateral exchanges between the United States and Japan. Out of necessity, she tapped the considerable talent of the Japanese students under her supervision, forming small groups of instrumentalists, singers, and dancers, which she arranged to perform at educational institutions. One of her students was performance artist Yoko Ono. In her autobiography, Beate tells of the young Yoko "giving demonstrations of calligraphy, the tea ceremony and origami at various functions."[1] Ono's first husband, the composer Toshi Ichiyanagi, played the piano in Beate's school programs.

Any time a Japanese artist of some renown passed through New York, Beate sought to get them involved

---

1 *The Only Woman in the Room, op. cit.,* p. 154.

in her programs, including the great koto player Kimio Eto, for whom she obtained from the composer Henry Cowell—a colorful figure of the American musical scene of the time (he had "prepared" the piano long before Cage did)—to write for him a concerto which was created by Leopold Stokowski conducting the Philadelphia Orchestra. Most importantly, she was adamant about bringing to the stage only the highest caliber performers, often in their first-ever US appearances including the illustrious Kyōgen performers of the famed Manzo Nomura VI troupe, who gave a number of exceptional performances in Europe and America in the 1960s.

In 1971, Japan Society constructed its own building— in modernist Japanese style designed by Junzō Yoshimura—near the United Nations headquarters on First Avenue. It was a beautiful space, encompassing a library, exhibition spaces, and a performance hall with some 260 seats built around an inner garden of water and bamboo. Previously, Japan Society had shared a space on Sixty-third Avenue with its sister organization, the Asia Society—also funded by Rockefeller. The Asia Society, which aspired to present the wider Asian world to the American public, covered a vast range of countries, reaching as far away as Australia, New Zealand, and the Pacific Islands. Since the two societies were spatially connected and—thanks to the Rockefeller constellation—structurally and financially linked, it did not take long for Beate to start working with both. In 1970, she took over the direction of Asia Society Performing Arts Department. She nonetheless continued to dedicate a good part of her time to Japan Society for roughly another decade. In 1981, Asia Society moved to its imposing new building on Park Avenue, endowed with a performance hall as spacious as that of its sister institution. From this point forward, until her retirement in 1991, Beate dedicated herself entirely to Asia Society.

Her mandate required that she produce three performances each year. One was usually from Japan, which still left a vast geographical and cultural area to cover—an entire artistic universe known until then to only a handful of Western scholars, and even then in a piecemeal and fragmented fashion. Beate traveled extensively each year to update the sparse information available on various troupes and to organize auditions (she categorically refused to invite artists unless she had personally seen their performances). Often she would return for a second review on the eve of the performers' departure for the United States, observing some sort of dress rehearsal in an effort to guarantee that the final product was what had been initially agreed upon.

For the most part, Beate traveled during the summer, covering five or six different countries in trips lasting up to six weeks. By the end of her career she had succeeded in visiting all of the twenty-two countries covered by the Asia Society mandate except Bangladesh, where her numerous attempts to visit were thwarted by an unfortunate series of ill-timed natural disasters.

Beate was an extraordinary storyteller, and she had a wealth of anecdotes about the numerous adventures encountered during her travels. She almost froze to death in a Mongolian yurt. She suffered altitude sickness over the high plateaus of Tibet and Bhutan. More than once, she found herself in close proximity to guerrilla warfare in the remote locations—hardly tourist destinations—while searching for unique and authentic performances by little-known ethnic minorities. In her colorful telling, she made even a simple road trip across Bengal—in which a sudden rainfall brought the multitudes sitting on the roof of the bus through the windows—sound like the journey of the damned!

All too often, Beate struggled to persuade national authorities to accept her vision and version of "traditional arts." Some did not appreciate the ancient and outmoded image they felt Beate was projecting of their country, particularly when her focus was on the art of marginalized minorities: groups either disregarded or held in outright contempt and suspicion by central powers. Even after overcoming official obstacles, she often faced challenges with the artists themselves; they would opt to use synthetic fabrics instead of their own traditional pure silk, or would "adjust" their traditional arts—already corrupted by the preferences of their own publics—to appeal to an imagined American public they believed would prefer a more "modern" version of their performance.

Once Beate confirmed the authenticity of a performance and scheduled American performance dates, she began the laborious task of preparing documentation commensurate with the educational aspirations of the organizers. Beate did not consider it sufficient that American audiences merely see and hear sublime and rare art. Rather, her primary desire was for these audiences to truly *understand* the deeper meaning of what they were observing. She was convinced that "an understanding of Asian culture could add a significant dimension to the education and enjoyment of every American."[2]

Beate strove to ensure that each performance at Asia Society would be educational and memorable. On the day of the premiere, the main event would be

2 The Asia Society, video cassettes, films, slides, publications, records, (1980s—exact date unknown).

preceded by a prologue in which the audience was invited to observe the actors' preparations for their performance—often set up in a separate space—thereby receiving an insider's view of the artists at work. The audience would, for example, witness at close range the physical metamorphosis of a frail-looking Indian actor into an imposing, statuesque, godlike figure as he applied the elaborate makeup and donned the colorful costumes in preparation for his Kathakali performance. In order to further enhance the experience, Beate often organized related cultural events, and arranged that the cuisine of the performers' home country would be served to audience members. For instance, meals available in Japanese Kabuki halls and preparations similar to bento boxes that the Japanese consume while viewing a performance were presented at intermission to American audiences during Japanese performances.

Beate also took great care to create the right atmosphere at each performance, so that American audiences would experience something close to what spectators would have experienced in the performers' home country. Considering that—in their original form—most performances would have taken place outdoors in natural settings, they rarely required any special stage sets or effects when transplanted in America.

Still, Beate's professional zeal for authenticity occasionally led to unexpected (and sometimes smelly!) situations. Having seen an outdoor performance of the indigenous populations of Sakhalin—a large island just north of Japan in the Far East Soviet Union—Beate requested at one event that dried fish be arranged around the stage during the American performance to match what she had seen overseas. Unfortunately, the effect didn't work well on an indoor stage. The fish left such an insufferable smell that the whole area had to be cleared with formaldehyde!

For the pleasure and edification of future audiences, Beate strived to preserve the legacy of the performances she produced. Through her efforts, the entire collection of the performances to which she had dedicated almost forty years of her life have some form of documentation. Under her supervision, twenty-nine videos and five films based on the events she had organized were produced for Asia Society. Nine recordings were released by Nonesuch Records, under the label's celebrated world music Explorer Series. The complete works, distributed widely among public libraries, universities, and art schools, today constitute a major collection of traditional Asian performing arts, at a crucial turning point in their transition to the modern era.

In 1991 Beate turned sixty-nine. It was time to bid farewell to her work. During her tenure, she organized more than forty different tours—each with some twenty to twenty-five performances presented at Asia Society and at various universities around the country. The Asian artists visiting under her auspices had traveled to more than four hundred cities in forty-two American states, and the performances were attended by more than 1.5 million Americans.

In a July 1991 article entitled "Asian Gifts," Deborah Jowitt, dance critic of the *Village Voice*, paid Beate a beautiful tribute:

> Beate Gordon, for 17 years the sensitive, wise, and innovative head of Asia Society's Performing Arts Program, retired last week to acclaim and a wealth of loving tributes. At a celebration honoring her, Kazuo Ohno, the legendary Japanese Butoh artist, danced for her in his tux—hilariously, movingly—to Sinatra singing "I Did It My Way." For years of great Asian performances, we can be grateful that she did it her way. For us all.

The stage director Peter Sellars would pay Beate—whom he considered a legend—a similar, and more personal, tribute. He once confided to her that he had had no experience whatsoever of Asian

performing arts until the day he had seen a performance organized by Beate at the University of
California in Los Angeles. He said that it had simply
changed his life.

An Interview with Beate Sirota Gordon

The following are extracts from the interviews conducted with Beate Sirota Gordon (BSG) March 8–10, 2012 at her New York apartment by Nassrine Azimi (NA) and Michel Wasserman (MW). The segments selected relate to the three main themes of the book, namely (I) the life and destiny of Leo Sirota, (II) the drafting of the Japanese Constitution, and (III) the presentation, to the American public, of the theaters of Asia.

I

MW: You know . . . when we talk about [Erich Wolfgang] Korngold and other musicians like him— they were always longing for their past in Vienna, and regretting the fact that they had had to go abroad. You did not have this impression with your father?

BSG: No, never. My mother wanted to go back to Europe, all the time. My father loved it in Japan. He really loved the Japanese, he felt very well, very comfortable with the Japanese, in every way. And his pupils adored him. Of course there was always something at the Academy, sometimes there were some difficulties with the director or with one of the other teachers, that's inevitable, but never anything that was a scandal as far as my father was concerned because he just was not that sort of personality, he had a very optimistic point of view, and I mean so optimistic, overly optimistic, for example that he did not believe that there could ever be a war between the United States and Japan, that it was absolutely out of question as far as he was concerned. He didn't think that this would ever happen, that Japan would ever, ever go into a war with the United States knowing how powerful the United States was. And so . . .

MW: This is why he came back?

BSG: Pardon me?

MW: This is why he came back in '41.[1]

---

1 Leo and Augustine had traveled to the United States in July 1941 to visit their daughter. *See* p. 51.

BSG: That's right, he did not believe there would be a war . . .

MW: Even at that time?

BSG: Even at that time. I know, my mother was crying and begging him to stay in the United States, and I was asking him to stay, and everybody, his friends, I think at that time Korngold was in . . . I'm speaking of '41, I think Korngold was in . . .

MW: He was in Hollywood.

BSG: In Hollywood. And we went to Hollywood for about a month and stayed there, he saw his friends there. I think we rented the apartment of Eva Le Gallienne.[2]

MW: I don't know her.

BSG: She was an actress in the United States, I'm not sure, she probably originally came from Europe, and we stayed there for about a month, and he saw his friends, and everybody was saying, you know, war is inevitable, that was in September through October of

---

2 Eva Le Gallienne (1899–1991), an American actress of British descent.

1941, people were talking like that, and my father would say: "Oh no, the Japanese never would dare attack a country like the United States." He was convinced that there would be no war. And my mother, of course, was not going to let him go back to Japan alone. I remember her weeping and crying and begging him to decide to stay, but I think he found that the life that the people like Korngold were leading in the studios . . .

MW: Was miserable?

BSG: Was very difficult, maybe miserable to some extent. He liked . . . he loved his students, he liked the much more leisurely pace in Japan than what he had found in the United States. And also [there was] more possibility of good work that he could do in Japan. That's how he felt. So he went back without any misgivings, with a wife who was full of misgivings as they went back. And then when they arrived, he was almost put in jail in Tokyo because somebody had reported that my father had taken some diplomatic documents to the United States with him when he had come to visit me, and that he had mailed a letter to [Edvard] Beneš and one to [Jan] Masaryk, given to him by the Czechoslovak . . . he was the Chargé d'Affaires in

Tokyo, Mr. [F.] Havlicek.[3] He was a very good pianist and a pupil of my father's. And before my father left. . . . My father was a very innocent sort of man politically speaking, the Chargé d'Affaires asked if he would be kind enough to mail two letters after he arrived in the States, and this was 1941, and in an envelope he had these two letters and he gave them to my father.[4] My father did not even look at them, but they were in his suitcase and he was going to open the envelope in San Francisco and just mail the letters, but it must be that somebody on the ship, a steward or somebody, found those letters in my father's baggage, I'm sure they went through the baggage of all people going to America at that time. My father went on the *Tatsuta Maru*, last time I think that a ship bearing silk was going. . . . The *Tatsuta Maru* was actually stopped in San Francisco Bay, and they were there, my mother and father were on the ship for about three days . . .

MW: Yes, and he played piano for the passengers. . . .

BSG: . . . to calm the people. But anyway some steward must have found those names and reported to the

---

3 *See* note 1, p. 33.

4 In her account, Beate's mother, Augustine, gives a slightly different rendition of the incident, suggesting that the letters had actually been confided to her, rather than to Leo. *See* p. 33.

Military Police in Japan, so when my father arrived back in Japan they wanted to put him in jail but the father of his pupil, Haruko Fujita, was an international lawyer. Haruko Fujita was my father's favorite pupil, a young woman who later on became the librarian at the Diet, and her father was an international lawyer, and he vouched with his life that my father was not a spy, and that it was a completely innocent act of his to have sent those letters off in San Francisco. So he was let off. My father did not go to jail.

MW: Yes, anyway he could . . .

BSG: That was already December 1941.

MW: Yes, and he was able to work, at least as a teacher and as an instrumentalist until late '43.

BSG: Yes.

MW: Did they talk a lot about Karuizawa afterwards?

BSG: To me?

MW: Yes.

BSG: Oh yes. It was very hard, because my father was not supposed to teach Japanese students, so my mother instead taught the children of the embassy people who were in Karuizawa.

MW: She was allowed to do it?

BSG: She was his assistant, she was allowed to do it, yes, but that was to foreigners, not to Japanese. My father could have taught foreigners also, but there were no foreigners of the type that would want to take piano lessons with my father. The people that my mother taught were children of embassy personnel, you know, whatever people, Europeans, were there in Karuizawa, so she taught, but my father wanted to barter some sweaters and woolen things and so on for food, and the Japanese were not supposed to have anything to do with foreigners in bartering things like that. But my father. . . . do you know that story?

MW: No, I don't think so.

BSG: My father liked to bicycle, and also in the woods he would cut firewood, and once he found a nice farm, he knocked at the door and asked the farmer whether he would be willing to barter things that he had, sweaters and shoes and so on that he would like to barter for food, and the man at first said, oh, no, no, we are not allowed to barter, then he looked at my father for a while and he said: Would you come into the house for just a moment, I want you to see something. So my father took off his shoes and went inside the house, and there, in the *tokonoma*[5] was a poster of my father from Hibiya Hall.[6] This particular farmer had been on one of these sight-seeing trips in Tokyo, and he had wandered around Hibiya Hall late in the evening when it was just about the end of a concert and he had never heard a piano before and he went in, the doors were not locked yet, you know, and he heard some music there and he went in, and he heard my father play and then he asked one of the ushers whether he could have the poster because he was so impressed, and so he took the poster and he kept it, and so when he realized that my father was the man on the poster he decided to barter with him, and gave him food for whatever my father offered.

MW: Your father in a way thought that he had been cheated by the Japanese?

---

5 A built-in alcove in traditional Japanese houses, where items of decoration are usually displayed.
6 The *Hibiya Kôkaidô*. *See* p. 23.

BSG: During the war?

MW: Yes.

BSG: He felt very, very strongly that he was badly treated. And that . . . but there were the people, different from the Military Police and government people . . . like his own pupils who did many, I would say heroic things for him, like when *Asama-yama*[7] exploded once all the glass of the cottage was shattered, it was not a Japanese-style house, but a summer house, and now all the windows were broken. One of his pupils from Tokyo came with her mother with broad glass, and cut it and put in into the windows, and then another pupil once brought a chicken and left it on the front steps of the house. So with his pupils in a secret way he still had some communication, very little but some, and some of them as I said helped him out, but he was very bitter about having been deprived of being able to teach. They had Japanese food rations, and that was not enough for a Westerner to live on, so my father got very, very thin. He suffered from malnutrition as did my mother. My mother blew up from malnutrition, my father got very skinny. Yes, he was very bitter about that, and then in

---

7 Mount Asama. *See* p. 27–28.

the last minute, about a week before the atomic bomb was dropped, the Military Police, who used to visit them I think almost every day to ask them questions during those two years whatever that they were there, and they said that they would arrest him and put him in jail, that he should get prepared and in a week they would come. And in that week the atomic bomb was dropped. So, of course, they never came to get him. The Minister of Education himself came to my father's house in Tokyo after the war to beg him to stay. But my father wouldn't stay, and then he went to the United States. But his last farewell tour, which took place when he was . . .

MW: Eighty or something . . .

BSG: Seventy-eight years old. He did go, but at that time he had been seventeen years in Saint Louis, almost as long as he had been in Japan. His Japanese pupils got together and invited him to come, and he did go. And I understand that it was the most moving thing. I couldn't go, I had two small children at that time and I couldn't go.

MW: Did he speak Japanese?

BSG: My father? No, he didn't speak . . . a little bit, *sukoshi dake, hontô ni sukoshi dake.*[8] My mother didn't speak Japanese either, also very little. And I think I mentioned in my book that she spoke kitchen Japanese. For example to take plates away from the dining table . . .

MW: Oh yes, *Sara sayônara!*[9]

BSG: *Sara sayônara*, that was the extent of my mother's Japanese . . . She spoke a little more than that, but she did not really speak fluently . . . I usually was the interpreter for her.

---

8 In Japanese: "Just a little, really, just a little."
9 *Idem.* Literally, "Sayonara, plates!"

II

BSG: The people, the Japanese public, seemed to express great satisfaction with the constitution.

MW: You mean the general people?

BSG: Yes, but the government was not very happy with it. But as I said we argued a lot, we started at ten o'clock in the morning and we finished . . . we finished not at two o'clock in the morning, mine was not the last clause to be discussed, it went on until five or six o'clock in the morning.

NA: The next morning.

BSG: Yes, and then Joe and his staff stayed on for language differences because they played around with language too. We tried to, you know, lower the powers of the Emperor and the Japanese did not like that, so they tried very hard when we were discussing the Imperial clause, to strengthen the words that gave power to the Emperor, and we argued again, that was a long discussion, it took a long time. We finally won out but there were some changes made. So the government was not, not enough, of course not happy with it, well, how could they? In the beginning, MacArthur hadn't wanted us to write the constitution, he had wanted the Japanese government to write it, and Joji Matsumoto, who was the minister without portfolio, who was supposed to write it, wrote a constitution that was so similar to the Meiji constitution you could hardly tell the difference. And then MacArthur said no, we could not accept it and asked Matsumoto to do it again —and again he came out with something that was completely impossible. That's when MacArthur decided . . .

NA: We are going to do it.

BSG: . . . that now we would actually go into our way of doing it because it was otherwise so impossible. . . . You see, he was worried that the Far Eastern . . .

NA: Commission.[10]

BSG: Commission, yes, was going to be having a meeting soon, in February, end of February I think,

10 The Far Eastern Commission (FEC), a joint Allied decision-making entity in Washington, had the mandate to oversee the American government and, by extension, General MacArthur. It had under its supervision the Allied Council for Japan, based in Tokyo and meant, in principle, to provide advice to MacArthur. MacArthur's distaste for any form of interference by the Allies in Japan and the beginnings of the Cold War, however, made this Council practically inoperative.

and he was afraid that there would be people there who would be wanting the Emperor to be declared a war criminal, because there were countries that wanted that, most of them the Allies. . . . The FEC was a committee that had to do with the governing of Japan, but, of course, MacArthur governed, and he had an Allied committee underneath him, but you should have seen how they were treated, I mean how badly, no information given to them, and oh, it was . . . I did not go to the meetings after a while because I was so embarrassed.

NA: But they were also in the same Dai-Ichi Building?[11] They were given a little corner of it?

BSG: You know, I wonder now whether they were or not, or whether they were outside, because I remember they were so looked down upon, I don't even remember whether they had a place, you know. I only saw them at the meetings and they had no power whatsoever. MacArthur was afraid that the FEC, if they met in February, would vote for the removal of the Emperor. He thought China would have voted for that . . .

NA: Russia . . .

---

11 *See* p. 58.

BSG: Russia, and Australia, I think, also, MacArthur didn't want that to come up, so he wanted the constitution *in situ*, before the meeting, already done, you know, *fait accompli*, because once you had a constitution then that was the law of the land. So that's why we had to do it so quickly, that's why the nine days.

NA: And what was the atmosphere like in SCAP[12] overall, I mean, what do you remember, was it . . .

BSG: During this period ?

NA: During this period, and generally during the time you were working, the eighteen months, was it exciting, was it . . .

BSG: It was very exciting, but the most exciting no doubt was when we started working on the Constitution . . . . it was exhilarating to see that about twenty people who were working on it, who had been enemies a few months earlier, who are now trying to plant the seeds of democracy, and elated to do it, and happy to do it, trying to push it, you know, to fruition. And that was really exhilarating, and we worked day and night because obviously nine days is a very short time, and using the

---

12 *See* p. 56.

constitutions that I had gathered from the different libraries. Everybody borrowed them because nobody had written a constitution before, they all were very happy to have something as a guideline, and so the constitutions were very helpful because they contained very good ideas, especially for women. They were very good guidelines, and . . .

NA: I remember you had the Soviet constitution, Bismarck . . .

BSG: Scandinavian constitutions.

NA: . . . Scandinavian . . .

BSG: . . . and Bismarck, and . . .

NA: American constitution . . .

BSG: Of course, American constitution, but it was interesting and to me at least surprising to see how many good things for women there were in both the Soviet constitution and in some of the Scandinavian constitutions. And so we worked as I said day and night because there were committees for each chapter of the constitution, a different committee. It couldn't possibly have been done altogether because there was too little time. One committee, my committee, was on the rights of the people, and there was one on the Emperor, there was a committee of three or four people, five people who worked on that, and there was another committee, for all the . . . every chapter had a different committee. And then . . .

NA: This is February 1946 . . .

BSG: Yes. This is in 1946. Then it went through the Diet and was promulgated by the Emperor.

NA: So, barely two months after you started working at SCAP you were already . . .

BSG: That's right, actually not even two months, about a month. I think I started about January 1 because I arrived late in December, and February 4 was the first meeting of our Committee.

III

BSG: I went to Purulia[13], which is in India, to see the Chhau dancers. Chhau[14], spelled C-H-H-A-U, crazy language. Anyway, we got into the forest of Purulia, and the trip itself was quite something, during the monsoon and all that, and our car stopping because the motor had water on it, I don't know whatever, but we finally get there around five o'clock in the afternoon, and the head of the Forestry Department was in charge at the forest we went to, in Purulia, and he's there and he says: Oh, all your dancers have gone home because we've been waiting here for you for six hours, and then they all went home. And I said: I came all the way from the United States to see this, it was one of the things I was going to see, and they are gone, well, use of the car and send people after them. When did they leave? Oh, they left half an hour ago. I said well, they can't be very far and he said well, they walk, but they walk into the mountains, and the road is good only for another mile, after that there are no roads and I said: Well, you've got to do something, you've got to send runners or whatever it

---

13 City in the state of West Bengal, with Calcutta as its capital.
14 Traditional dance from East India. Performed outdoors at night by men as part of the spring ritual. Its movements evoke combat, stylized behavior of animals, as well as scenes of daily life of villagers. The Chhau dance unfolds in three distinct styles specific to different regions—the one of Purulia being by far the most acrobatic and spectacular.

is because I have got to see it, I came here, even if we can only see them in the middle of the night I don't care. So they put us into what used to be . . . the British authorities had little sort of bungalows where the British overseers would stay, so one was reserved for us, I was there with an Indian anthropologist and his assistant, and we got in there, and the forest head said: Okay, we will send some people after them, some runners to bring them back, and in the meantime we stayed there and they brought us a parade of fishes from the outside, I don't know where they had their kitchen or whatever it was, and we ate and then it was getting very dark, there was only one light bulb in every room, there was a bed, but it had such a thin mattress you cannot imagine, and one sheet and no pillows. Anyway we all went to sleep and in my dream I heard drumming. I thought it was my dream, but I woke up and I heard the drumming again, and then I looked out the window, of course it was pitch dark in the middle of the forest, no lights anywhere, but I could hear drumming. So, there was no door between my room and the other guest room, just a little *volant*, there, that's all, and I said: Professor Bhattacharya[15], please wake up, I

---

15 Ashutosh Bhattacharya (1909–1984), Indian anthropologist, who in the 1960's "discovered" the dances of Chhau from Purulia—a region of vast forests, accidented terrain, and reputedly hostile local tribes, which made it particularly difficult to penetrate.

think I hear drumming, and so he woke up, and his disciple woke up, too, and they said yes, yes, you're absolutely right, it's drumming, let's go downstairs and we will have flashlights ready, and sure enough when these people came they had ladders, between two people there would be a ladder held horizontally.

MW: A ladder . . .

BSG: A ladder, a real ladder, and on each ladder was the headdress of what they wore during the . . . very elaborate headdress. And I was thinking: where are they going to show it to us, and the forest manager said: oh, it's just a little way to a clearing, and they can dance there. And when they started to drum more and more and more the people from the villages started coming out, because they could hear this only on festival days, once a year[16], and here they were hearing and seeing it out of season.

MW: And it was in the middle of the night?

BSG: In the middle of the night, it was at five o'clock in the morning that they came. So, anyway, they are coming out with babies on their backs and all that.

---

16 In the first half of April, to celebrate spring and the renewal of agriculture.

MW: There were lights? Torches?

BSG: They had torches and flashlights, that's all.

MW: And they came to demonstrate?

BSG: They came to audition, yes, forty of them came. So we all woke up of course, and we went there, and then all these people around, from nowhere, coming out from the earth it seemed like. And then they danced, and it was very, very, very interesting, very fantastic kind of dancing. When they were finished, our car driver said: we have to hurry because I have to take you to the airport to go to Sri Lanka, so we have to hurry, please get your things ready. And we got our things ready, but I saw that Mr. Bhattacharya was in a little cubicle there, in that house, he was sitting there and all the dancers were coming in, and he was doing something, and I didn't know what he was doing with them. What he was doing was taking their fingerprints as a receipt for the money that I was paying for the audition, so that later on the authorities would not be bothered by other people in the village saying how come these people have money and we don't have anything, and so that they could prove with the fingerprints of these that they had been paid for an audition, it was all of two dollars, I want you to know, per person. And then we're getting on the plane, Mr. Bhattacharya says to me: I will try to keep them alive for you. The dancers. I said: Excuse me? He said: Inevitably there is a famine and so on, many people will die, but I will bring them food from Calcutta. And I said: Oh, I would like to send something, what can I send from the States, powdered milk, you know, things like that or whatever that they needed, and he said: Oh, that will be very good, if you send the money I can buy it and bring it to them. And he said: You have chosen a certain number among the dancers, he said that's another reason why I needed these receipts, because you know, money is life or death. And so I went on the plane and said to myself: My God, I chose among the forty, I chose fourteen to come. And to be in a situation to have chosen people, and out of them these fourteen are going to live and who knows what is going to happen to the others who are left. That's a terrible thing to think about, it haunted me for a long time, you understand obviously . . .

MW: Because you mean the guy would pay attention for the fourteen, and the other ones . . .

BSG: Because they were not in the troupe, you see. Terrible . . .

NA: Yes, and it's still haunting you because you talked to me about this.

MW: You wrote about it in your book.

BSG: Oh, I did, I did ...

MW: This is I guess, for you it's number one story this one.

BSG: Yes, that was very, very traumatic.

NA: Striking.

MW: Don't you think that one of the great problems of these so called ... *minzoku geinô*[17] is that it is very hard to transplant to a western stage? I mean what you see, for instance, in nature I guess, and when you put it on a ...

BSG: Well, you see, now, I have a story about that, in Sakhalin, I saw them dancing outside in a field, and there was fish hanging on sticks to dry, like for *katsuo bushi*[18], you know.

---

17 In Japanese, "folkloric performance."
18 In Japanese, "dried bonito," one of the core ingredients of traditional Japanese cuisine.

MW: You went to Sakhalin too?

BSG: I went to Sakhalin. And I told my stagehand in New York I was going to get some fish, dry fish, and I want it to be hung on the stage on poles, just plain old poles, and we went to the fish market with the Sakhaliners. When the Sakhaliners arrived in New York City, the first thing I did is to go to Chinatown with them to buy the fish. And you've been to Chinatown, masses of things, masses of things, but in Sakhalin, when a store had something like potatoes it might have only potatoes that day, nothing else. And everybody in the village would go to buy these potatoes, and there was nothing else to buy. So we come to Chinatown with those masses of things, and we go to buy fish, and they want to buy souvenirs, and I said: I'm sorry, we have no time for that. And in the subway, we all went by subway, because there were so many of them I did not want to lose them, they are making very dark faces you know, like this. I'm speaking to the Russian inter-preter, I said: Why are they in such a bad mood? And he said: It is because you would not let them buy any souvenirs. And I said: But I told them that we could come another day, and we would buy them. And he said: who knows whether anything would be left? Isn't that a wonderful story? In Chinatown! You never forget that.

NA: They did go back, so that, of course . . .

BSG: Of course they did.

NA: That it was still there.

BSG: They did go. Also they went to Macy's, and went crazy at Macy's.

A Tribute
by Nicole Gordon[1]

Minasama konnichiwa[2].

Thank you for your introduction. Our many sincere thanks to the organizers of this moving event. I thank the audience members and Beate's good friends who are here today.

Beate's family—her grandchildren Lara and Sam, and my husband Roger and I who are here—as well as my brother Geoffrey and my daughter Danielle who are in the US—thank you all for your deep affection for Beate during her lifetime and beyond. Beate was a true citizen of the world, but her heart and spirit were always with Japan and with the Japanese people.

---

1 On March 30, 2013 Beate's daughter Nicole took part in a memorial in Tokyo, in honor of her mother, and gave this speech.
2 In Japanese, "Good morning, everyone."

I want to tell you how Beate worked for the Japanese people right up to her death.

As you know, having grown up in Japan, Beate, by incredible chance, had the remarkable opportunity to work on the Japanese Constitution while she was still a young woman of twenty-two.

She was the "right person at the right time" to do this, knowing the language, culture, and people of Japan intimately as only someone who has grown up in this country could.

She contributed to the Japanese Constitution in several ways.

First, having drafted the women's and civil rights and academic freedom sections.

Second, having the foresight and familiarity with Tokyo to look for and find foreign constitutions that she and other staff could use as models for GHQ's work.

Third, she worked as an interpreter—the "only woman in the room"[3]—during the negotiations between the Americans and Japanese on the final version of the constitution.

And finally, much later when secrecy was lifted, she worked tirelessly as an advocate for the Japanese Constitution.

---

3 Title of Beate's memoir, *The Only Woman in the Room*, *op.cit.*

For more than thirty years Beate did not speak about her role because it was classified information, and she feared that the facts that she was young, a woman, and not a lawyer would be used to discredit the Constitution. But I will say that I am now fifty-eight years old, and I am a lawyer. I say with great pride but also as a professional: I could not dream of doing as good a job as she did even with almost forty years of professional experience. She had something more important than a law degree. She really knew and loved Japan, and she had the sensitivity and experience to articulate what was needed.

In between the late 1940s and the early 1990s, she had a professional life in the US and devoted herself to international cultural exchange, particularly in performing arts, working at the Japan Society and the Asia Society. She brought many performing artists from Japan and Asia to tour in the United States. She believed that if people of different nations understand each other better, they will be able to create a sustainable culture of peace. She put Geoffrey and me to work helping with timing the performers, running the tape recorder, and preparing programs. We attended performances of virtually every artist she brought to the US. And now my brother is a playwright and an actor.

Many people in the United States were profoundly influenced by seeing the performances of the artists across the spectrum from the traditional Awaji Bunraku, Bugaku, and Kagura to such contemporary artists as Hanayagi Suzushi[4], Ohno Kazuo, Eiko and Koma[5], Satô Sômei[6], and Kazenoko[7] whom Beate brought from Japan and from more remote countries. She was completely open-minded and admired all styles and all kinds of art—as long as it was authentic and first-rate. In her career, she also worked with many famous artists of Japan including Nagare Masayuki[8], Tange Kenzô[9], Kusama Yayoi[10], Ono Yôko—who arranged for Geoffrey and me to go to a recording session of the Beatles (the greatest day of our lives!)—and above all her dear, dear friend Munakata Shikô.

---

4 Classically trained dancer and choreographer, who also mastered contemporary creations (1928–2010). She collaborated with Robert Wilson for years, who called her his "teacher" and was always indebted to Beate for connecting them.

5 Duo of contemporary dancers, based in New York.

6 Composer, born in 1947, whose work incorporates many elements of traditional Japanese music.

7 Or "Children of the Wind," a theatrical troupe founded in 1950 that performs mainly for children.

8 Sculptor born in Nagasaki in 1923. Has worked in Japan and abroad on many large-scale public pieces, one of which disappeared in the terrorist attacks on the World Trade Center.

9 Renowned figure of Japanese contemporary architecture and winner of the Pritzker Prize (1913–2005). He designed the Hiroshima Peace Memorial Museum.

10 Plastician artist, born in Matsumoto in 1929. She was one of the precursors of pop art and environmental art, and worked for years in New York with Andy Warhol and Claes Oldenburg.

It was hard for Beate when she had to retire in 1991 from the work at the Asia Society that she was so dedicated to. But around that time, luckily for her, her role in drafting the Japanese Constitution became widely known.

So suddenly after her retirement she had a new career that brought her back often to her beloved Japan. It gave her a new life and she was thrilled to be active in her great cause for the Japanese people. She became sought after to speak about the history of the Constitution and as a public, vigorous advocate for its preservation, especially the women's and civil rights and peace clauses. She gave lectures—the bigger the audience the better—wrote a book in Japanese and English, was the subject of documentaries and even of a play. Every public appearance was a joy to her.

My mother was a very social person. She loved talking with artists, activists, and scholars. She always told my father what time she would come home, but she was always one or two hours late because she could not tear herself away from a conversation. And he was always furious about it!

She became ill almost a year ago. She did not talk about her illness even with close friends. She stayed strong to take care of my father, Lt. Joseph Gordon, who was chief of the interpreters section at GHQ. It was here in Tokyo in the Dai-Ichi building that they met in 1945. He died at home on August 29th, 2012 at the age of ninety-three. She died also at home at eighty-nine, almost exactly four months later, on December 30th, of pancreatic cancer.

Earlier in December, the *Asahi Shinbun* had asked her for an interview about the Japanese Constitution. The paper did not specify at first when the interview should be. Beate knew that there was talk of amending the Japanese Constitution; of course she believed that the Japanese Peace Constitution—far from being a document that needs to be changed—should rather serve as a model for all other countries. She knew she was dying, and she was determined to seize this opportunity to make her last, strong statement supporting the Japanese Constitution in a highly public and influential forum.

She was no longer seeing people or even speaking on the telephone (which she had always loved to do!). But we arranged an interview to be done by telephone and, if necessary, in writing via e-mail that I would type for her.

She dictated two paragraphs to me to read to the reporters in response to questions the newspaper had posed. This was in case she was too weak to answer the questions herself when the time came. I gave her the typewritten paragraphs in the evening. In the morning I was surprised to see that she was making corrections as she lay on her side in bed. I did not think she would have the strength any more even to do that. She was bed-ridden, getting weaker every day.

Even so, I came into her room on a Tuesday to see that after many days not having left her bed she was sitting up, dressed to be ready for a telephone interview. But there was a misunderstanding about the date, and the interview was not scheduled until Thursday.

And indeed, by Thursday, she did not even try to get up on the day of the interview. Although the interview was scheduled for the afternoon, she asked me to place the call to the newspaper in the morning, because she was afraid she was losing the physical ability to speak at all. She used her last strength for this interview, to speak one more time—emphatically in favor of preserving the Japanese Constitution. Beate hoped to encourage people in Japan working for peace.

This was just ten days before she died. It was truly her final effort.

She died knowing that she had done literally everything she could to support the Japanese people through her work on the Constitution. She had finished her work.

After she died, newspapers and Internet sites from all around the world carried obituaries describing her work on the Constitution. And in Japan, well over one hundred articles have appeared about her since she died. She would have been so happy to know that in this way she helped the cause of preserving the Japanese Constitution even after her death. It was more than she could possibly have imagined; and it is certainly what she would have wished for. As my brother once pointed out, Beate always exceeded expectations.

When the US Congress had hearings about new constitutions for Iraq and Afghanistan, Beate was asked to speak about how to incorporate equal rights for women in those countries. She testified that the drafters of new constitutions should consult with the women of Japan, to learn what it means to have women's rights included in a Constitution and the difference that that can make in people's lives.

Our family appreciates how deeply you care for Beate's legacy. We know you will continue to teach young people about the history of Japan and the history of the women of Japan so that Japanese people of many generations will continue to protect women's rights and human civil rights and to work for peace.

When Geoffrey and I thought about the best way to honor Beate's memory, we decided that we should ask people, rather than sending flowers, to send support to the Article 9 Association[11] and work for peace.

I brought Beate's ashes to Japan so that a part of her, like her heart and spirit during her life, will always be in Japan—with a view of *Fuji-san*.

Arigatô gozaimashita[12].

—NICOLE GORDON
Tokyo, March 30, 2013

Nicole Gordon is Beate's daughter.

---

11 Association founded in 2004 by some of Japan's most renowned intellectuals, including Ôe Kenzaburô, winner of the Nobel Prize for Literature. Their aim is to defend the constitution from attempts at revision, in particular Article 9, by which "the Japanese people forever renounce war as a sovereign right of the nation and the threat or use of force as means of settling international disputes."
12 In Japanese, "Thank you very much."

An Elegy
by Geoffrey Gordon

YOU ARE FIVE YEARS OLD. YOUR father plays the piano, your mother gives parties. You are a dancer. The ship is sailing. The old world is gone. The new one speaks a different language. This is not a problem. You love language. You are a genius with words, but not as good with numbers.

You are fifteen, alighting on yet another new shore, this time in a country whose language you know, even though no one there can quite place your accent or pronounce your name. You excel.

You are twenty-two. All of your homelands have been to war with each other. Your passport says "expert." It is correct. You find your starving parents and save them, also there is a constitution to write. You are the only woman in the room. You work in secret for equality and peace. You succeed.

There is a man. He is uniquely suited to your taste. He is handsome, yes, but also funny, brilliant, kind, and like-minded. You marry forever. There are children. They are encouraged.

You do not follow a career path, you create one. You are an indomitable aesthete; peerless. You see through to the authentic expression. The true artists are your pride; you are their gift. This goes on for decades. You climb mountains, fly helicopters, and dine with the hunters of heads. You make the indigenous international. You constellate your stars and see how they shine! Then some number of years has suddenly passed and you are . . . silenced!

But it does not last: you are not shy, you are not retiring. You dance on. There are grandchildren. You show them the world. There is the book and newfound fame from what you accomplished half a century before. There are appearances, signings, symposia, colloquia, etc., etc., etc. . . . There are films, plays, events, articles, hearings, and talk shows. You thrive.

You have more years than there are keys on the piano. There are no more parties. But there is love all around, and veneration. You give one last interview. It takes all of your strength. Now the world is singing your name, out loud and to itself; it feeds from your inspiration. We hear the echoes of your call to excellence. Your legacy is the art of living in beauty and truth, of speaking up and out for what is right, and of finding our best selves and sharing them.

You were five years old. Your father played the piano, your mother gave parties. You were a dancer. The ship is sailing. The old world is gone. The new one speaks a different language. This is not a problem. You love language. You are a genius with words. You will understand. They are shouting: "Brava, Beate, brava!"

—GEOFFREY GORDON
April 28, 2013

Geoffrey Gordon is Beate's son.

Preface
to *Post-Conflict Reconstruction*[1]

THE RECONSTRUCTION OF COUNTRIES AND THAT of
peoples' lives after war continues to be one of the most
pressing and momentous tasks before us, and the
speakers and panelists at the UNITAR Hiroshima
Conference in November 2002 have each eloquently
presented diverse perspectives on this challenging
endeavour. I will therefore limit myself in this note to
my own experiences with one part of the reconstruction in post-Second World War Japan, namely the
drafting of the new Japanese Constitution.

In February of 1946, Douglas MacArthur, Supreme
Commander, Allied Powers, ordered the Government
Section of the GHQ in Tokyo to produce a draft of the
new Japanese Constitution. I was assigned to draft the
women's rights articles. Most of the staff on our team

---

1 *Post-Conflict Reconstruction . . ., op. cit.*

were not specialists in constitutional law—rather they were civil servants, lawyers, professors of Japanese history, linguists, and economists, but we all knew how to do research, and we all had a fervent desire to be part of the changes unfolding in Japan. For guidance, we read as many constitutions as possible from other nations. Of course, we also had instructions from Washington and from the steering committee formed within the Government Section. In one week, we were able to produce a constitutional draft, which the Japanese writer James Miki described recently as "written by the wisdom of history."

The basic rights of women remain, regardless of what one may say about cultural differences, one of the pillars in the rebuilding of post-war societies. Before the Second World War, Japanese women had no rights— no right to marry or divorce by choice, no right of inheritance, no right of choice of domicile or property. Today as I work with many women's groups all over Japan and see their dynamism and energy, I can but wish that donor countries would always make their reconstruction assistance conditional on women's fundamental rights being spelled out in the new constitutions of countries emerging from war and tyranny.

The new Japanese Constitution has lasted for fifty-six years, without amendment, a first in world history.

The governments and peoples of the world which face the same situation as the Japanese did in 1945 might do well to study the new Japanese Constitution which, according to the scholar John Dower, has the most progressive civil rights clauses of any constitution of its time. It also has a peace clause, Article 9, which prohibits aggressive war. It is a pity that very few people in the world know about this, or about the many other lessons inherent in the reconstruction of post-war Japan. Countries such as Afghanistan and East Timor, emerging from conflict and struggling to give reality to their longing for peace, can learn many valuable lessons from Japan as they work through constitutional and other reforms. The Japanese Constitution's peace clause has been fully embraced by the Japanese people themselves, and has played a significant role in bringing the country economic prosperity due, in part, to the savings resulting from reduced military expenditure. Would that other countries adopted it!

On a more subtle level, since 1947, the Japanese Constitution has brought profound changes to the mores of a once militaristic society, and has sown the seeds of democracy and equality. Critics insist that because of cultural differences and customs, the Constitution is not "Japanese" enough. Japan's experience has demonstrated, however, that in the end, people around the world are far more alike than they are different. They all want freedom, food, good health, education for their children, and happiness. Universal human rights know no boundaries. And those of us who have the privilege of enjoying these rights also have a responsibility to help others achieve the same goals. We must do so with idealism, passion, and the will to prevail. The alternatives are simply too grim to contemplate.

—Beate Sirota Gordon

New York City, January 2003

Selected Segments of
the Japanese Constitutions of
February 11, 1889 and November 3, 1946

The Constitution of the Empire of Japan was promulgated on February 11, 1889. Inspired by the authoritarian Prussian constitution, it, too, was founded on monarchic principles and granted the subjects of the Empire limited personal freedoms. The Constitution of Japan, Japan's postwar constitution, was promulgated on November 3, 1946. It rejected the totalitarian nature of the Meiji constitution, renouncing war and ensuring a far greater protection of civil liberties. The following are the first sections of each document: the preamble, status of the emperor, the rights and responsibilities of the empire's subjects or state's citizens, and, for the 1946 constitution, the unique Article 9 on the renunciation of war.

Constitution of February 11, 1889

Preamble.

HAVING, BY VIRTUE OF THE GLORIES of Our Ancestors, ascended the throne of a lineal succession unbroken for ages eternal; desiring to promote the welfare of, and to give development to the moral and intellectual faculties of Our beloved subjects, the very same that have been favored with the benevolent care and affectionate vigilance of Our Ancestors; and hoping to maintain the prosperity of the State, in concert with Our people and with their support, We hereby promulgate, in pursuance of Our Imperial Rescript of the 12th day of the 10th month of the 14th year of Meiji, a fundamental law of the State, to exhibit the principles, by which We are guided in Our conduct, and to point out to what Our descendants and Our subjects and their descendants are forever to conform.

The right of sovereignty of the State, We have inherited from Our Ancestors, and We shall bequeath them to Our descendants. Neither We nor they shall in the future fail to wield them, in accordance with the provisions of the Constitution hereby granted.

We now declare to respect and protect the security of the rights and of the property of Our people, and to secure to them the complete enjoyment of the same, within the extent of the provisions of the present Constitution and of the law.

The Imperial Diet shall first be convoked for the 23rd year of Meiji and the time of its opening shall be the date, when the present Constitution comes into force.

When in the future it may become necessary to amend any of the provisions of the present Constitution, We or Our successors shall assume the initiative right, and submit a project for the same to the Imperial Diet. The Imperial Diet shall pass its vote upon it, according to the conditions imposed by the present Constitution, and in no otherwise shall Our descendants or Our subjects be permitted to attempt any alteration thereof.

Our Ministers of State, on Our behalf, shall be held responsible for the carrying out of the present Constitution, and Our present and future subjects shall forever assume the duty of allegiance to the present Constitution.

CHAPTER I.
The Emperor

Article 1. The Empire of Japan shall be reigned over and governed by a line of Emperors unbroken for ages eternal.

Article 2. The Imperial Throne shall be succeeded to by Imperial male descendants, according to the provisions of the Imperial House Law.

Article 3. The Emperor is sacred and inviolable.

Article 4. The Emperor is the head of the Empire, combining in Himself the rights of sovereignty, and exercises them, according to the provisions of the present Constitution.

Article 5. The Emperor exercises the legislative power with the consent of the Imperial Diet.

Article 6. The Emperor gives sanction to laws, and orders them to be promulgated and executed.

Article 7. The Emperor convokes the Imperial Diet, opens, closes, and prorogues it, and dissolves the House of Representatives.

Article 8. The Emperor, in consequence of an urgent necessity to maintain public safety or to avert public calamities, issues, when the Imperial Diet is not sitting, Imperial ordinances in the place of law. (2) Such Imperial Ordinances are to be laid before the Imperial Diet at its next session, and when the Diet does not approve the said Ordinances, the Government shall declare them to be invalid for the future.

Article 9. The Emperor issues or causes to be issued, the Ordinances necessary for the carrying out of the laws, or for the maintenance of the public peace and order, and for the promotion of the welfare of the subjects. But no Ordinance shall in any way alter any of the existing laws.

Article 10. The Emperor determines the organization of the different branches of the administration, and salaries of all civil and military officers, and appoints and dismisses the same. Exceptions especially provided for in the present Constitution or in other laws, shall be in accordance with the respective provisions (bearing thereon).

Article 11. The Emperor has the supreme command of the Army and Navy.

Article 12. The Emperor determines the organization and peace standing of the Army and Navy.

Article 13. The Emperor declares war, makes peace, and concludes treaties.

Article 14. The Emperor declares a state of siege. (2) The conditions and effects of a state of siege shall be determined by law.

Article 15. The Emperor confers titles of nobility, rank, orders and other marks of honor.

Article 16. The Emperor orders amnesty, pardon, commutation of punishments and rehabilitation.

Article 17. A Regency shall be instituted in conformity with the provisions of the Imperial House Law. (2) The Regent shall exercise the powers appertaining to the Emperor in His name.

CHAPTER II.
Rights and Duties of Subjects

Article 18. The conditions necessary for being a Japanese subject shall be determined by law.

Article 19. Japanese subjects may, according to qualifications determined in laws or ordinances, be appointed to civil or military or any other public offices equally.

Article 20. Japanese subjects are amenable to service in the Army or Navy, according to the provisions of law.

Article 21. Japanese subjects are amenable to the duty of paying taxes, according to the provisions of law.

Article 22. Japanese subjects shall have the liberty of abode and of changing the same within the limits of the law.

Article 23. No Japanese subject shall be arrested, detained, tried or punished, unless according to law.

Article 24. No Japanese subject shall be deprived of his right of being tried by the judges determined by law.

Article 25. Except in the cases provided for in the law, the house of no Japanese subject shall be entered or searched without his consent.

Article 26. Except in the cases mentioned in the law, the secrecy of the letters of every Japanese subject shall remain inviolate.

Article 27. The right of property of every Japanese subject shall remain inviolate. (2) Measures necessary to be taken for the public benefit shall be any provided for by law.

Article 28. Japanese subjects shall, within limits not prejudicial to peace and order, and not antagonistic to their duties as subjects, enjoy freedom of religious belief.

Article 29. Japanese subjects shall, within the limits of law, enjoy the liberty of speech, writing, publication, public meetings and associations.

Article 30. Japanese subjects may present petitions, by observing the proper forms of respect, and by complying with the rules specially provided for the same.

Article 31. The provisions contained in the present Chapter shall not affect the exercises of the powers appertaining to the Emperor, in times of war or in cases of a national emergency.

Article 32. Each and every one of the provisions contained in the preceding Articles of the present Chapter, that are not in conflict with the laws or the rules and discipline of the Army and Navy, shall apply to the officers and men of the Army and of the Navy.

Constitution of November 3, 1946

WE, THE JAPANESE PEOPLE, ACTING THROUGH our duly elected representatives in the National Diet, determined that we shall secure for ourselves and our posterity the fruits of peaceful cooperation with all nations and the blessings of liberty throughout this land, and resolved that never again shall we be visited with the horrors of war through the action of government, do proclaim that sovereign power resides with the people and do firmly establish this Constitution. Government is a sacred trust of the people, the authority for which is derived from the people, the powers of which are exercised by the representatives of the people, and the benefits of which are enjoyed by the people. This is a universal principle of mankind upon which this Constitution is founded. We reject and revoke all constitutions, laws, ordinances, and rescripts in conflict herewith.

We, the Japanese people, desire peace for all time and are deeply conscious of the high ideals controlling human relationship, and we have determined to preserve our security and existence, trusting in the justice and faith of the peace-loving peoples of the world. We desire to occupy an honored place in an international society striving for the preservation of peace, and the banishment of tyranny and slavery, oppression and intolerance for all time from the earth. We recognize that all peoples of the world have the right to live in peace, free from fear and want.

We believe that no nation is responsible to itself alone, but that laws of political morality are universal; and that obedience to such laws is incumbent upon all nations who would sustain their own sovereignty and justify their sovereign relationship with other nations.

We, the Japanese people, pledge our national honor to accomplish these high ideals and purposes with all our resources.

CHAPTER I
The Emperor

Article 1. The Emperor shall be the symbol of the State and of the unity of the People, deriving his position from the will of the people with whom resides sovereign power.

Article 2. The Imperial Throne shall be dynastic and succeeded to in accordance with the Imperial House Law passed by the Diet.

Article 3. The advice and approval of the Cabinet shall be required for all acts of the Emperor in matters of state, and the Cabinet shall be responsible therefor.

Article 4. The Emperor shall perform only such acts in matters of state as are provided for in this Constitution and he shall not have powers related to government. The Emperor may delegate the performance of his acts in matters of state as may be provided by law.

Article 5. When, in accordance with the Imperial House Law, a Regency is established, the Regent shall perform his acts in matters of state in the Emperor's name. In this case, paragraph one of the preceding article will be applicable.

Article 6. The Emperor shall appoint the Prime Minister as designated by the Diet. The Emperor shall appoint the Chief Judge of the Supreme Court as designated by the Cabinet.

Article 7. The Emperor, with the advice and approval of the Cabinet, shall perform the following acts in matters of state on behalf of the people:

- Promulgation of amendments of the constitution, laws, cabinet orders and treaties.
- Convocation of the Diet.
- Dissolution of the House of Representatives.
- Proclamation of general election of members of the Diet.
- Attestation of the appointment and dismissal of Ministers of State and other officials as provided for by law, and of full powers and credentials of Ambassadors and Ministers.

- Attestation of general and special amnesty, commutation of punishment, reprieve, and restoration of rights.
- Awarding of honors.
- Attestation of instruments of ratification and other diplomatic documents as provided for by law.
- Receiving foreign ambassadors and ministers.
- Performance of ceremonial functions.

Article 8. No property can be given to, or received by, the Imperial House, nor can any gifts be made therefrom, without the authorization of the Diet.

CHAPTER II
Renunciation Of War

Article 9. Aspiring sincerely to an international peace based on justice and order, the Japanese people forever renounce war as a sovereign right of the nation and the threat or use of force as means of settling international disputes.

In order to accomplish the aim of the preceding paragraph, land, sea, and air forces, as well as other war potential, will never be maintained. The right of belligerency of the state will not be recognized.

CHAPTER III
Rights and Duties of the People

Article 10. The conditions necessary for being a Japanese national shall be determined by law.

Article 11. The people shall not be prevented from enjoying any of the fundamental human rights. These fundamental human rights guaranteed to the people by this Constitution shall be conferred upon the people of this and future generations as eternal and inviolate rights.

Article 12. The freedoms and rights guaranteed to the people by this Constitution shall be maintained by the constant endeavor of the people, who shall refrain from any abuse of these freedoms and rights and shall always be responsible for utilizing them for the public welfare.

Article 13. All of the people shall be respected as individuals. Their right to life, liberty, and the pursuit of happiness shall, to the extent that it does not interfere with the public welfare, be the supreme consideration in legislation and in other governmental affairs.

Article 14. All of the people are equal under the law and there shall be no discrimination in political, economic or social relations because of race, creed, sex, social status or family origin. Peers and peerage shall not be recognized. No privilege shall accompany any award of honor, decoration or any distinction, nor shall any such award be valid beyond the lifetime of the individual who now holds or hereafter may receive it.

Article 15. The people have the inalienable right to choose their public officials and to dismiss them. All public officials are servants of the whole community and not of any group thereof. Universal adult suffrage is guaranteed with regard to the election of public officials. In all elections, secrecy of the ballot shall not be violated. A voter shall not be answerable, publicly or privately, for the choice he has made.

Article 16. Every person shall have the right of peaceful petition for the redress of damage, for the removal of public officials, for the enactment, repeal or amendment of laws, ordinances or regulations and for other matters; nor shall any person be in any way discriminated against for sponsoring such a petition.

Article 17. Every person may sue for redress as provided by law from the State or a public entity, in case he has suffered damage through illegal act of any public official.

Article 18. No person shall be held in bondage of any kind. Involuntary servitude, except as punishment for crime, is prohibited.

Article 19. Freedom of thought and conscience shall not be violated.

Article 20. Freedom of religion is guaranteed to all. No religious organization shall receive any privileges from the State, nor exercise any political authority. No person shall be compelled to take part in any religious act, celebration, rite or practice. The State and its organs shall refrain from religious education or any other religious activity.

Article 21. Freedom of assembly and association as well as speech, press and all other forms of expression are guaranteed. No censorship shall be maintained, nor shall the secrecy of any means of communication be violated.

Article 22. Every person shall have freedom to choose and change his residence and to choose his occupation to the extent that it does not interfere with the public welfare. Freedom of all persons to move to a foreign country and to divest themselves of their nationality shall be inviolate.

Article 23. Academic freedom is guaranteed.

Article 24. Marriage shall be based only on the mutual consent of both sexes and it shall be maintained through mutual cooperation with the equal rights of husband and wife as a basis. With regard to choice of spouse, property rights, inheritance, choice of domicile, divorce and other matters pertaining to marriage and the family, laws shall be enacted from the standpoint of individual dignity and the essential equality of the sexes.

Article 25. All people shall have the right to maintain the minimum standards of wholesome and cultured living. In all spheres of life, the State shall use its endeavors for the promotion and extension of social welfare and security, and of public health.

Article 26. All people shall have the right to receive an equal education correspondent to their ability, as provided by law. All people shall be obligated to have all boys and girls under their protection receive ordinary education as provided for by law. Such compulsory education shall be free.

Article 27. All people shall have the right and the obligation to work. Standards for wages, hours, rest and other working conditions shall be fixed by law. Children shall not be exploited.

Article 28. The right of workers to organize and to bargain and act collectively is guaranteed.

Article 29. The right to own or to hold property is inviolable. Property rights shall be defined by law, in conformity with the public welfare. Private property may be taken for public use upon just compensation therefor.

Article 30. The people shall be liable to taxation as provided by law.

Article 31. No person shall be deprived of life or liberty, nor shall any other criminal penalty be imposed, except according to procedure established by law.

Article 32. No person shall be denied the right of access to the courts.

Article 33. No person shall be apprehended except upon warrant issued by a competent judicial officer which specifies the offense with which the person is charged, unless he is apprehended, the offense being committed.

Article 34. No person shall be arrested or detained without being at once informed of the charges against him or without the immediate privilege of counsel; nor shall he be detained without adequate cause; and upon demand of any person such cause must be immediately shown in open court in his presence and the presence of his counsel.

Article 35. The right of all persons to be secure in their homes, papers and effects against entries, searches and seizures shall not be impaired except upon warrant issued for adequate cause and particularly describing the place to be searched and things to be seized, or except as provided by Article 33. Each search or seizure shall be made upon separate warrant issued by a competent judicial officer.

Article 36. The infliction of torture by any public officer and cruel punishments are absolutely forbidden.

Article 37. In all criminal cases the accused shall enjoy the right to a speedy and public trial by an impartial tribunal. He shall be permitted full opportunity to examine all witnesses, and he shall have the right of compulsory process for obtaining witnesses on his behalf at public expense. At all times the accused shall have the assistance of competent counsel who shall, if the accused is unable to secure the same by his own efforts, be assigned to his use by the State.

Article 38. No person shall be compelled to testify against himself. Confession made under compulsion, torture or threat, or after prolonged arrest or detention shall not be admitted in evidence. No person shall be convicted or punished in cases where the only proof against him is his own confession.

Article 39. No person shall be held criminally liable for an act which was lawful at the time it was committed, or of which he has been acquitted, nor shall he be placed in double jeopardy.

Article 40. Any person, in case he is acquitted after he has been arrested or detained, may sue the State for redress as provided by law.

Afterword
by Sonia Sotomayor
Associate Justice, Supreme Court of the United States

I MET BEATE GORDON THROUGH HER accomplished daughter Nicole Gordon, with whom I had had the pleasure to work on the establishment of public financing of New York City elections in the 1980s. During many social functions at Nicole's home, Beate, was always present. Simply looking at the twinkle in her eyes, I knew that there was something very special about this highly charming, cultured, and gracious woman. It was not until I had the good fortune to read her fascinating memoir, *The Only Woman in the Room*, that I realized that the exceptional daughter, Nicole, was the product of an even more exceptional mother.

As many of you may know, Beate lived in Japan with her parents for over ten years as a child. She came to the United States by herself for her secondary education when she was not yet sixteen years old. After World

War II, she returned to Japan to work as an interpreter for the military and to look for her parents, whom she eventually found. In her interpreter's role, she won the hearts of both the Japanese and American representatives drafting the new Japanese Constitution and convinced them to do something extraordinary. She persuaded them to include two provisions in the new Constitution that the United States Constitution lacks to this day. Articles 14 and 24, which the delegates included at her urging, guaranteed equality between men and women, prohibited discrimination on the basis of sex and required mutual consent for and equal treatment in marriage.

What a path-breaking woman Beate was at such a young age. But this was only the beginning. She spent the rest of her life advocating for women's rights and promoting cultural understanding between Japan and the United States.

There are many people who live in foreign lands and never make the effort to understand and become part of the cultures of the places they live. Beate was not one of those people. Having lived in two nations far from her Austrian birth, Beate adopted both Japan and the United States as her own. She loved them, and did everything in her power to open the door of understanding and appreciation between the cultures of each of her adopted countries. Others today will speak in more detail of her extensive work bringing Asian performing arts to the United States and her efforts as a women's rights advocate. It suffices for me to say that it takes a special kind of person to have lived life with so much passion, and given to two countries as much as Beate did.

I felt privileged in having gotten to know Beate. It is rare life treat for a Supreme Court Justice to get to meet a framer of a Constitution. It is rarer indeed for that framer to have been a woman. More importantly, however, Beate helped teach me how to live fully in two cultures, and make both my home. I suspect that just as I say that I am an American with a Puerto Rican heart, Beate was an American with a Japanese heart.

The world has lost a special star in Beate's passing, but the legacy of friendship and understanding she left behind will immortalize her spirit.

—SONIA SOTOMAYOR
Associate Justice of the Supreme Court of the United States
April 28, 2013

From a transcript of commentary presented during the 2013 celebration of Beate's life and legacy at Asia Society.

About the Authors

 NASSRINE AZIMI HAS CO-FOUNDED AND NOW coordinates the Green Legacy Hiroshima (GLH) Initiative, a global campaign to plant worldwide seeds and saplings of trees that survived the atomic bombing of Hiroshima in 1945. She was the founding director of the Hiroshima Office for Asia and the Pacific, United Nations Institute for Training and Research (UNITAR), in 2003. Previously she had served as the first coordinator of the Institute's environmental training programs, deputy to the executive director, and chief of the Institute's New York Office. Azimi has written and published extensively on training, UN peacekeeping, post-conflict reconstruction, architecture, and environmental governance. She has a post-graduate degree in urban studies from the School of Architecture of the University of Geneva, an MA in international relations from the graduate Institute of International Studies, also in Geneva, and a BA in political science from the University of Lausanne.

She lives in Hiroshima.

MICHEL WASSERMAN IS THE FORMER
DIRECTOR of the Kyoto French Cultural
Institute and of a French "artist in residence"
program in Kyoto, the Villa Kujoyama. He
is currently Professor at the College of
International Relations, Ritsumeikan
University. A Paris III doctor in oriental
studies, Michel Wasserman has worked and written
extensively on Japanese traditional theater, especially
kabuki, and has also published various books on the
reception of western music in Japan. For the last decade,
he has been involved in a research on the Japanese
period of the "Poet-Ambassador" Paul Claudel, who
played a decisive role in promoting Franco-Japanese
bilateral relations during the twenties: *D'or et de neige—
Paul Claudel et le Japon* (Éditions Gallimard), was
awarded the 2009 Émile Faguet Prize by the Académie
Française, and won that same year the "Prix Littéraire
de l'Asie."

He lives in Kyoto.

Photos